CARS THAT
TIME FORGOT

CARS THAT TIME FORGOT

Giles Chapman

PARRAGON

First published by Parragon 1997

© Parragon 1998

Parragon
13 Whiteladies Road, Clifton,
Bristol BS8 1PB, United Kingdom

Designed, produced and packaged by
Stonecastle Graphics Ltd.,
Old Chapel Studio, Plain Road, Marden,
Tonbridge, Kent TN12 9LS, United Kingdom

Edited by Philip de Ste. Croix

Page 1: The aggressively beautiful Jaguar XKSS. Page 2:
Panther Deville – king-size but ersatz. Page 3: Hanomag
'people's car' weaving its way along a modern hillclimb.
Above: Aston Martin Bulldog set for (aborted) take-off.

ISBN 0-75252-539-5

Printed in Italy

Photographic credits

All photographs courtesy of **Giles Chapman**
with the exception of the following:
Neill Bruce: 1, 2, 4, 7 (*below*), 13, 14, 15 (*main picture*), 38 (*below*), 44 (*top*), 45, 64, 77 (*top*),
91, 92 (*below*).
**The Peter Roberts Collection c/o Neill
Bruce:** 6, 10 (*top*), 18 (*top*), 24 (*top*), 28 (*top*),
35 (*top*), 69 (*below*), 75 (*below*).
Brian Smith, Daimler Owners' Club: 37.
Chris Willows, BMW: 3, 20, 38.
Byron Garages International: 60 (*top*).
Haymarket Archives: 16 (*top*), 21, 24
(*bottom*), 42, 48, 56/7, 62, 71, 74, 79, 84/5.
N. Wright/National Motor Museum: 7 (*top*).

Contents

Introduction

THE VOLKSWAGEN Beetle, the Ferrari F40, the McLaren F1, Jaguar's E-Type, Model T Ford, Morris Minor, Chevrolet Corvette, Porsche 911, the Mini of course, the Mercedes-Benz SL. Some of the truly great names in cars, I'm sure you'll agree. Immortal, almost. And also some of the most thoroughly documented.

Even the most casual of car enthusiasts knows that you could have a Model T in any colour as long as it was black, or that the McLaren F1 is easily the fastest road car in the world.

Well, this book is an antidote to all that. It's a collection of some of the most fascinating waifs and strays that the motoring world has ever, metaphorically speaking, abandoned on the great freeway of life; cars that, while they might have seemed like the bee's knees when they were dreamed up, were quickly engulfed in the swirling mists of time and obscurity.

After all, for every Beetle or Mini, there are dozens of hopefuls that never make it to the automotive Hall of Fame.

Good ideas at the time? Glorious failures? Broken dreams? Hopeless innovations? Intrepid entrepreneurs? They, and more, are all here. But the one thing that binds them together is that, for one reason or another, they've all been forgotten while the Corvettes and E-Types of this world have remained as gleaming nostalgia on wheels. Nevertheless, I trust that, as you turn the pages, there are one or two that make you say 'Oh yes, *I* remember that' or 'So *that's* what it was'.

Below: The 1973 Owen Sedanca, Britain's failed attempt to build a Lamborghini Espada rival. Right, above: Was the Tucker really torpedoed by the industry big guns? Right, below: John Weitz's decidedly unfashionable X600.

'After all, for every Beetle or Mini, there are dozens of hopefuls that never make it to the automotive Hall of Fame.'

As a writer and journalist I've always been intrigued by dreamers and design mavericks, idealists and inventors. You probably remember John De Lorean and his infamous DMC-2 gullwing car – maybe even Preston Tucker and his amazing rear-engined Torpedo. They've both been immortalized on the silver screen, the former with Michael J. Fox in the *Back to the Future* series, the latter in its own movie, *Tucker: The Man and His Dream*.

Let's face it, cars on their own are only *so* interesting, no matter how fast they go or how much they cost – it's individuals and stories that bring them alive. And whenever I read anything about wacky car people, or the sometimes bizarre fruits of their endeavours, I carefully tear the story out of the newspaper or magazine and keep it. If I come across a fuzzy photo of a car I don't recognise I can't rest until I've found out all about it.

For me, this book has been a marvellous chance to gather together, for your delectation, some of the most unusual, amusing and, I suppose, sorrowful motor cars and their creators ever in one place. Come with me for a rummage through my 'Filing Cabinet of the Damned'!

If you like stories about human endeavour, you should find a lot here to entertain you. And if you're just plain nuts about cars, I hope there are things here you've just never clapped eyes on before.

Most of all, if you come across a car that leaves you totally baffled, let's be hearing from you . . .

Giles Chapman
London, England, 1997

Alfa Romeo Arna

WHEN TIMES are hard, people resort to desperate measures. And like an aristocrat reduced to selling timeshare apartments, Alfa Romeo was up against it in the early 1980s. It was owned by the Italian state, but the investment it needed to finance replacement of the Alfasud and its other old faithfuls was scarce.

A marriage with Nissan appeared to offer a dream solution. The 1984 Arna was the first born offspring.

This transplanted the front suspension, engine and gearbox of the Alfasud into the body of the Nissan Cherry. The car was assembled at Alfa's plant near Naples and sold in Europe as either the Arna or the Nissan Cherry

Europe. Alfa purists may have hated the ugly shape and typically Japanese interior but, as it was lighter than the Alfasud, it was rather quicker – especially in 1.5Ti form – with handling not much worse than its illustrious forebear. But it was never what you'd call popular.

After less than five years, though, the marriage was over: Fiat bought the ailing

> ‘Alfa purists may have hated the ugly shape and typically Japanese interior.’

Alfa Romeo and hoisted the all-Italian flag above it once more. Nissan built its own factory in Sunderland, And the Arna was quietly consigned to history.

Nissan body but wheels and grille hint at Alfa heart.

Allard Clipper

SYDNEY ALLARD, bespectacled garage owner and sports car maker from Clapham, south-west London, won the 1952 Monte Carlo Rally, the only man to do so in a car of his own design. But even as the champagne corks flew from their bottles in Monaco, fast cars from big companies, especially Jaguar, with their superior refinement and performance, were obliterating sales of small-time specials like Allards.

'What resulted was one of the ugliest British bubble cars ever.'

Optimistic sales material (left) extolled the economic virtues of the diminutive Allard Clipper — note how far out of scale the people are to make the tiny car look absolutely enormous! However, it wasn't so much 'indestructible' as unsaleable, and production got no further than a pilot batch of 20 cars, of which this (below) is a rare survivor owned by Graham Deakin.

Sydney's answer was to attack the other end of the scale – he planned to produce the ultimate economy car. He employed a young engineer called David Gottlieb to design it and a firm called Hordern-Richmond Ltd to make its plastic body.

What resulted was one of the ugliest British bubble cars ever, a tiny egg-shaped contraption that could seat three abreast in cramped discomfort and a further two children in 'dickey seats' behind when the boot was converted.

An 8bhp, 346cc Villiers twin motorbike engine powered the car via its nearside rear wheel. But cooling difficulties and weak driveshafts meant the Clipper, besides looking ludicrous, was also hopelessly unreliable.

A pilot batch of about 20 were made but, despite Syd's cheerful exhortation to 'Take the nipper in a Clipper', real production never got underway.

Today, there are just two survivors, one in Germany and this one – which, according to owner Graham Deakin, was apparently so undesirable it had nine owners between 1955 and '62, including one garage that had it returned three times by disgruntled buyers!

AMC Pacer

'In living memory, few new cars have received such derision upon their debut.'

DURING THE fuel crisis of the mid-1970s American car makers were stymied. GM, Ford, Chrysler and AMC (American Motors Corporation) just didn't make small, fuel-efficient, economical cars, and they looked on aghast as Japanese imports piled in and snatched sales.

The panic to compete sired some emergency products: the Ford Pinto, which later developed a tendency to ignite in accidents; the Plymouth Cricket, a hastily imported and 'Americanized' Hillman Avenger; and the AMC Pacer.

Ah, the Pacer! In living memory, few new cars have received such derision upon their debut. Britain's *Motor* magazine, for instance, announced on its cover 'We test the Pacer – and wish we hadn't'.

In photos, the goldfish-bowl looks and three doors suggested a car that was VW Polo-size. In the metal, it was longer than a Ford Granada, with the huge wheels of every other Detroit dinosaur.

Above: When it was new, people couldn't quite believe the Pacer. Below: Collector status could beckon for surviving cars.

As an economy model, you would probably expect a thrifty engine. But the smallest available in the Pacer was a burly six-cylinder 3.8-litre motor as big as a Jaguar's.

It did boast a driver's door longer than the passenger's for easy access to the rear seats. But even that novelty went pear-shaped when cars were converted to right-hand drive for the UK market.

The Pacer utterly failed to stave off the challenge from the Toyota Corolla and its dainty ilk and lasted a miserable five years before AMC quietly snuffed it out. Today, if you own an Edsel, a perfectly preserved Pacer makes an ideal companion . . .

Anadol

'By 1970, over 10,000 had been bought by proud Turks.'

FOR TURKEY, where national pride runs high, the first all-Turkish car was never going to be some Western cast-off. However, without any car-manufacturing heritage or, indeed, much industrialization of any sort, Turkey couldn't produce one from scratch.

Unlikely assistance came from Reliant, Britain's three-wheeler maker and, during the late 1950s and early '60s, purveyor of 'instant motor industries' to places like Israel and Greece.

Reliant provided the design (a small family saloon, Ford Escort-sized), the technology (how to make glass fibre and bend and weld steel tubes into a chassis), the know-how (planning the Istanbul factory) and the nuts and bolts (crates of Ford engines and other parts assembled, packed in the UK and shipped east).

In 1966, the first Otosan Anadol was announced and, by 1970, over 10,000 had been bought by proud Turks. An Anadol similar to the one shown here

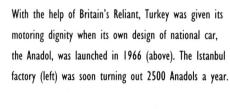

With the help of Britain's Reliant, Turkey was given its motoring dignity when its own design of national car, the Anadol, was launched in 1966 (above). The Istanbul factory (left) was soon turning out 2500 Anadols a year.

even won the local 917km (570-mile) Thrace Rally, to prove its national worth.

It wasn't until 1984 when the Anadol was very decrepit indeed, that Otosan acknowledged modern times . . . by buying the tools to make the old Ford Cortina, which it did until 1993 when it was replaced by the latest Escort. However, an Anadol pick-up was made until 1991.

Aquila

'Chris Field's rather severe looking, five-door Aquila was the favourite.'

IN 1972 and '73, the *Daily Telegraph* was itself a big pull for car fanatics at London's Earl's Court Motor Show. The newpaper's colour magazine, then published every Friday, organized the construction of two unique cars in an attempt to highlight the work of young British car stylists.

With the help of the Institute of British Carriage & Automobile manufacturers, the magazine's editor, the late John Anstey, devised the first competition heat in 1971. A design brief for a smart two-door coupé was set, and a young Rootes stylist called Michael Moore won with a neat fastback called 'Cirrus'. His prize was to receive the finished car at the following year's motor show.

Based on a standard Escort saloon donated by Ford, Cirrus was built by a hearse maker in Halifax, Yorkshire and contained a host of other parts begged and borrowed from British components makers, in exchange for the hoped-for publicity, like Lucas, Triplex and Smiths Industries.

For 1972, the competition brief was for a family saloon car of the future (to be launched in 1976) based on the Austin Maxi, and Chris Field's rather severe looking, five-door Aquila was the favourite, British Leyland this time providing the car.

Although there were plans to continue the British Styling Competition throughout the 1970s, the cost was prohibitive – Cirrus cost £16,000 to

make, Aquila reputedly £26,000. The *Telegraph* bowed out when it became clear that the motor industry's benevolence in terms of encouraging new styling talent was, in reality, wafer-thin.

Happily, both the unique Cirrus and Aquila cars still exist in the hands of enthusiastic owners.

Chris Field's sketches (above) and ideas were deemed good enough to make the Aquila (below) a reality.

Armstrong Siddeley Station Coupé

'Most of the few examples built went to Australia.'

ARMSTRONG SIDDELEY has never exactly been a name to conjure with in the car world. Created in 1919 by the merger of similarly double-barrelled rivals Armstrong-Whitworth and Siddeley-Deasy, it made cars until 1960, after which it stuck to manufacturing aero-engines.

Its cars were solidly-built, of decent quality but, dare I say it, a tad dull.

Still, Armstrong Siddeley stole a march on everyone in 1945 when it was the first British manufacturer to launch brand new post-war cars. The Lancaster saloon and Hurricane coupé offered 2-litre six-cylinder engines, a pre-selector gearbox, and new era looks.

The series lasted until 1954 in various forms but the oddest versions were the two-seater Station Coupé (pictured) and three-seater Utility Coupé. Both were a cross between a car and a truck, with

Possibly one of the most stylish pick-ups ever made, the Armstrong Siddeley Station Coupé's utilitarian nature still made it a popular choice in Australia and New Zealand.

graceful lines hiding roomy pick-up space at the back.

Most of the few examples built went to Australia and New Zealand, where 'utes' were every outbacker's dream, but their genteel British heritage made them a poor match for the durable, rough and ready Fords, Holdens and Jeeps that ruled the rocky roost down under.

Aston Martin Bulldog

IN 1980 the Aston Martin V8 and Vantage looked ever more like outdated grandfather clocks next to the slim, modern timepieces with which rivals Ferrari and Lamborghini were stunning the motoring world. The Bulldog, although it still had that British tick-tock to its name, was Aston's riposte.

More wedge-shaped than a powerboat, and packing Aston's handmade V8 engine amidships behind the driver's shoulder, the Bulldog's two giant doors opened from the centre of its low-slung roof like a seagull's wings. Inside, although the rich leather and thick carpet were traditional enough, the car was thoroughly futuristic, with a rear-view TV monitor and a built-in loudhailer.

Stylist William Towns was responsible for its rocket ship design but he was not happy with how the car was made – especially when he found that road grime dripped on to his clothes from the edges of the open doors when disembarking in wet weather.

The fully roadgoing Bulldog, said its maker, could nudge 290km/h (180mph) and was a star turn at 1980 motor shows. Alas, by then, such sharp-edged design

'Two giant doors opened from the centre of its low-slung roof like a seagull's wings.'

was becoming passé and no Aston as radical as this has appeared since. The present owner Cliff Baron from Essex has refused £1.2m for this unique car.

The Bulldog was about as far from the traditional Aston image as it was possible to get, but its 'gullwing' doors (opposite, inset) made entry and exit a bit hazardous...

Austin 3-litre

'The result must be judged as one of the most ungainly cars of the 1960s.'

YOU MAY recall that Sir Alec Issigonis was the creator of the Morris Minor, the Mini and the Austin/Morris 1100 – the car that John Cleese once famously thrashed in an episode of *Fawlty Towers*. A chain-smoking engineering genius, Issigonis never married, said in public that he hated America and all he thought it represented, and produced cars that, while brilliant in their concepts and always spacious, were often somewhat spartan alongside market-led rivals like Ford and Vauxhall.

His Austin and Morris 1800 cars were typical – long on space, short on showroom appeal and, unlike Ford Granadas and Vauxhall Victors, slow sellers. At least the Maxi, using an identical passenger compartment and doors but with the versatility of a hatchback at the rear, was a better prospect. But not by much.

The most bizarre, and least successful, of Issigonis's cars, however, was the Austin 3-litre. Again utilizing the middle section of the 1800, this lumbering giant had a 2.9-litre straight-six cylinder engine shared with the MGC.

Too long to fit across the car to give the front-wheel drive Issigonis preferred for its smaller siblings, the 3-litre had a longer nose to house the engine and rear-wheel drive, a configuration that ate into the brilliant designer's roomy cabin. The result must be judged as one of the most ungainly cars of the 1960s, despite such technically interesting features as air suspension at the back.

In a double misunderstanding of the mentality of the average luxury car buyer, BMC decided to call the poor thing an Austin, rather than use the more upmarket Wolseley, Riley or Vanden Plas

Below: Perhaps the best view of the massive 3-litre was from behind, where it looks almost graceful. Bottom: An early car, featuring the never-produced oval headlights.

names held in its portfolio of marques. It was the kiss of death; just 9992 examples were sold between 1967 and 1971 – that's fewer than 2000 a year.

Austin A40 Countryman

'Apart from the Range Rover, few other cars have adopted the A40's horizontally-split hatch.'

IT WAS not long ago that the Austin A40 was a common sight on British roads. Although it was born in the 1950s and shared many of its unseen parts with the even older A35, the Austin A40 had a long and happy production life, with more than 340,000 made until its demise in 1967.

It was the Metro of its day, and in more ways than you might think, because the 'Countryman' version was the first ever hatchback.

There had been cars with an opening 'tailgate' before, such as the Citroën Traction Avant and Aston Martin DB2. But none had the A40's neat 'two-box' shape – one box for the engine and another for the passengers and luggage – which today is almost universal.

Apart from the Range Rover, few other cars have adopted the A40's horizontally-split hatch, with the bottom metal half dropping down and the upper glass part swinging skywards.

Unfortunately, though, the A40 has never been a car of much panache, even though its crisp styling, by Pininfarina, seemed the height of modernity in 1958. The similarly sized Ford Anglia and Triumph Herald, while neither as innovative nor as versatile, possessed the charisma that the A40 lacked.

The vast majority of A40 Countrymans have already been scrapped, and more will undoubtedly follow until the call to save this British pioneer is heeded.

Novel design made the A40 the first true 'hatchback'.

Avanti

'The car is still available – now as a convertible and even as an outrageous stretched limousine.'

A MERICA'S AVANTI is beginning to take on Britain's own Morgan for venerability. Vaunted in 1962 when it was announced by Studebaker, the car is still theoretically available some 35 years on. Its creator, designer Raymond Loewy, however, had become accustomed to his work attaining 'immortality' by the time he died in 1986.

The man who virtually invented industrial design single-handedly – when he stylishly clad the Gestetner duplicating machine – is outlived by such designs as his classic Coca-Cola bottle, Lucky Strike cigarette pack and the NASA Skylab space station interior.

His sharp and unadorned lines for the glass fibre-bodied, supercharged V8 Avanti were instantly hailed by a country weaned on Detroit's steel behemoths.

The unfortunate Studebaker itself was bankrupt by 1964, but two of its dealers, Nate Altman and Leo Newman, bought the old South Bend, Indiana factory and continued to make 100 'Avanti IIs' each year. Although the enterprise has

changed hands since, the car is still available – now as a convertible and even as an outrageous stretched limousine – if you really still want one after all this time. Its car-crazy designer, Loewy, would have been chuffed.

Raymond Loewy was a life-long car fanatic, so it was inevitable he should take a break from designing photocopiers and company logos to have a go at something four-wheeled. That the Avanti (below), originally a Studebaker (above) is still with us is a tribute to his timeless touch.

BL ECV3

'The car boasted the internal space of a Ford Mondeo in a package little bigger than a Metro.'

THE ENGINEERS were quick to make a point about ECV3: their third Energy Conservation Vehicle was never destined to cut you up on city ring roads or appear on a used car forecourt. It was not, repeat **not**, going into production.

As if to prove the point emphatically, the next showroom debutante from the company, then called BL, was the dreary Austin Maestro.

ECV3, by contrast, was the company's three-dimensional, fully working – and all-British – engineering exercise to design a lightweight, economical car of the near future.

Its entire body structure was made from bonded aluminium, a strong alloy frame incorporating roof and sills, with clip-on plastic panels. The boffins acknowledged that these would be more costly than steel but pointed to the fact that they weighed a third less than traditional metal, helping ECV3 achieve an average fuel consumption figure of

Above and below: The sleek styling of BL's third Energy Conservation Vehicle hid some clever engineering, an aluminium frame with plastic body panels that simply clipped into place. It was never destined for the streets.

22km/litre (63mpg). They pointed out that, for every 1 per cent reduction in car mass, there was an extremely worthwhile fuel saving of 0.3 per cent.

Other notable features were a three-cylinder engine, flush-fitting windows to aid the aerodynamic shape – drag co-efficient was an incredible 0.25 – and special, lightweight brakes.

The car boasted the internal space of a Ford Mondeo in a package little bigger than a Metro. Although BL, later Rover, was forced to adapt Honda designs for its next generation of cars, experience gleaned from ECV3 was used to spectacular effect in Rover's K series engine – itself a design award winner. The car still exists and you can examine it at Rover's museum at Gaydon near Birmingham, just a few yards from where it was constructed in 1982.

BMW 700

'The performance was plodding, with 30bhp of power allowing a 113km/h (70mph) top speed.

FROM BEHIND the wheel of your 3 or 5 Series you might find it hard to relate to the BMW 700. It was, after all, shorter than the Triumph Herald which it at first glance resembles (they were, after all, both styled by the same man, Italy's Giovanni Michelotti).

It had a 700cc engine in the back where BMW drivers would today sling their golf clubs or suitcases; this meant that engine noise was mostly out of earshot, and it needed to be because the twin-cylinder, motorbike-derived unit was a tad rowdy. And the performance was plodding, with

The neat BMW 700 is the forgotten link between BMW's bubble car period and today's super-successful range.

30bhp of power allowing a 113km/h (70mph) top speed.

However, just like today's 3 Series, a choice of saloon, coupé or convertible was available and, as with today's M3, you could have more power if you wanted it: the twin carburettors of the CS and Sport models meant they were good for 129km/h (80mph) with better acceleration. In this guise they put up a

plucky showing in their class of saloon car racing in the early 1960s.

In the preceding decade, BMW had been primarily a motorbike and bubble car maker, and had felt the chill wind of financial disaster. While the 1500 saloon of 1961 really hauled BMW back from the brink, the unassuming 700, of which 188,000 were sold from 1959 until 1965, provided the vital financial lifeline.

Breutsch Mopetta

PICTURE THE scene: London's Earl's Court in October 1956, and Breutsch Cars England, squashed into a corner of a motorbike show between the scooters and the pudding-bowl crash helmets, has just unveiled the world's smallest car, the Breutsch Mopetta.

No, this isn't an unfeasibly large man at the helm of the Breutsch Mopetta – the car really is that small! What a shame it never caught on...

Herr Egon Breutsch was a monied German racing driver convinced that the world badly needed miniature motoring, and the Mopetta was one of some half-dozen attempts by him to put his ideas into practice – two of the others are keeping the Mopetta company here.

The Mopetta really was tiny, just 170cm (5ft 7in) long, 88cm (2ft 11in) wide and weighing 61kg (134lb) with a single seat that you lowered yourself into rather as you would into an old-fashioned tin bath. Its rotund form half-hid a 49cc moped engine that bulged out of the left side just in front of the rear wheel, which it drove singly.

Macho bikers doubtless chortled at this tiny three-wheeled eggcup: Breutsch, meanwhile, had sealed a deal with Georg von Opel of the eponymous German car maker to mass-produce it, but only a few 'Opelit Mopetta' prototypes were made.

Although one of the least successful car makers of all time, Breutsch later emerged as one of Stuttgart's pre-fab building barons. The 1956 show car, amazingly, is still alive and well in an English collector's garage.

'Macho bikers doubtless chortled at this tiny three-wheeled eggcup.'

Citroën 2CV Metro

T'S A SIMPLE beast, the Citroën 2CV, its two cylinders clattering and its body leaning wildly to left or right on even the most gentle of bends. Low on acceleration and even meaner on petrol consumption. But it could never, ever be called modern

It had been introduced in 1948 as no-frills rural transport for the most cash-strapped of French peasant farmers and, while enduringly trusty, it belonged to another, slower age.

On safety grounds alone, it's right down there with rotating combine harvester blades and two-bar electric fires on damp bathroom floors.

All of which makes this bizarre 1975 confection even more incredible: the Metro was an attempt to fly in the face of

'On safety grounds alone, it's right down there with rotating combine harvester blades.'

Under the aristocratic nose of the Metro (below) lurked a GS engine but Citroën wisely decided that go-faster stripes were the most suitable performance accessory for the original car (right).

modern cars like the Volkswagen Golf and Alfasud, and keep the 2CV alive for even longer.

This gentrified version, with its chintzy fake hood irons, chrome grille and fancy wheels, came with twice the punch of the usual, snail-like 2CV – under its bonnet was the flat-four cylinder Citroën GS engine.

Thankfully, good sense prevailed and Citroën let the humble 2CV see out its days without suffering the hot-rod treatment, while developing proper modern cars like the Visa and BX for up-to-date tastes.

Citroën Bijou

'The Bijou was heavier than the original, puny 2CV, and so even slower.'

I N THE shadow of the home of the chocolate *Mars* bar in Slough, Bucks, Citroën assembled a version of its rustic French 2CV between 1953 and '59 for the British market. To make the bizarre car acceptable to British eyes, Citroën fitted chrome bumpers and hubcaps, covered the hammock-type seats in plaid cloth, and stuck a badge on the front saying 'Citroën Front Drive'. Buyers, though, stayed away in droves. They bought nice, normal Standard Eights and Austin A30s instead.

The plastic-bodied Bijou (below) weighed more than the 2CV it was based on. The car's brochure (bottom) tried to present the car as an ideal partner for modern living.

In a last-ditch attempt to force the 425cc, two-cylinder 2CV on us, Citroën produced a unique British 2CV. The 1959 Bijou featured a 2CV chassis with a smart new glass fibre body from the drawing board of Peter Kirwan-Taylor – the stylist of one of the best-looking contemporary new cars, the Lotus Elite.

Alas, the handiwork was fine but the Bijou was heavier than the original, puny 2CV, and so even slower. And the new Mini easily undercut the £674 Bijou. In five years, just 207 of this, the only Citroën ever designed outside France, were sold.

Britain happily took to the 2CV when it was re-introduced in 1974 . . . at the height of an acute energy crisis.

Citroën LN

'It shoved the clattering twin-cylinder engine from the 2CV-based Dyane into the hull of a two-door Peugeot 104.'

IF YOU'VE seen the new Citroën Saxo you might have noticed that it looks uncannily like the Peugeot 106. So you won't be surprised to learn that they share the same wheelbase, engines, gearboxes and suspension as well. Citroën is Peugeot-owned.

The days are long gone when small Citroëns were quirky, noisy, ungainly looking things that commanded respect and contempt in equal measure. The new small Citroën is a cheap-to-develop, blandly acceptable, identikit hatchback. Eminently practical, nippy and thrifty, but a clone of countless other similar designs nonetheless.

It's a policy that's not new to Citroën. Some 20 years ago, in 1976, in a similar effort to cut design corners, it shoved the clattering twin-cylinder engine from the 2CV-based Dyane into the hull of a two-door Peugeot 104 and christened it the Citroen LN. Later models, called LNA, even stuck with the four-cylinder 104 engine. Only the badges and a few insignificant details were different.

The LNA was sold in the UK for a few years. An undistinguished and forgotten car, the task of identifying one was made even harder with the 1981 arrival of the Talbot Samba. Although the trained eye might have spotted the different rear wings and grille, it too was a 104 in all but name.

And was the Peugeot 104 itself a bad car? Not really. But it was, you know, just another car.

Above: You could easily mistake the little LN for a Peugeot 104 or Talbot Samba — in fact, the three were near-identical, especially when later LNs adopted the four-cylinder Peugeot engine for added zip (below).

Dacia Denem

I T DOESN'T matter how dull a motor car may seem to novelty-hungry European eyes, there will always be a market for it somewhere. So it is that spent-force models that we thought had shuffled off this mortal coil have often, in fact, sneaked away for a new life in far-flung places.

The Dacia is one Romanian orphan that's managed to survive pretty well, even if it is, to Western Europe, little more than a cast-off Renault 12. Attempts to sell it to Britain as the Denem (below), however, were a failure.

The Renault 12, for instance, was a terminally tedious, albeit mostly very dependable, machine last made in France in 1980.

However, it has survived and indeed flourished in Romania as the Dacia. The Romanians started assembling 12s in 1972 but, while France progressed to other, more exciting models, Dacia saw no reason to change.

In fact, the Dacia has mutated, like a seeded onion in the Eastern European

sunshine, into forms never imagined by Renault designers: there are now pick-up, van, hatchback and even coupé versions of the 12 on offer.

A half-baked plan to import the car to the UK, as the Dacia Denem, in 1982 was a failure – apart from a small fleet which is still in service with the Romanian embassy in Kensington. The advertising didn't help much: the car was touted as the 'Very acceptable Dacia Denem'. Most enticing.

'A half-baked plan to import the car to the UK, as the Dacia Denem, in 1982 was a failure.'

Daihatsu Trek

'Designed specifically to turn the average 10-year-old quadbike addict back into a boy scout.'

THE POPULAR idea might be etched on your mind that Japanese car makers have got where they are today by copying what Europe and America already did so successfully. But these days you can hardly accuse them of being mere mimics. Ther's a real spirit of innovation in their industry.

Every two years, the Tokyo Motor Show throws up more wacky ideas and quirky design concepts than you'd find at a dozen American motor shows.

Funnily enough, Daihatsu, one of Japan's smaller makers, begets more than its fair share of 'concept' cars.

Here's one from around 1990 which was designed specifically to turn the average 10-year-old quadbike addict back into a boy scout.

The Trek, with its single seat, rugged construction, reassuringly sturdy roll-over bar and high ground clearance would certainly have been a lot of fun off-road.

However, should junior have found himself too far away from home at night to get back again, the steering column dropped down, the seat folded shut and the Trek became a comfy single bed.

Mosquitoes or downpours? No problem: simply pop up the instant tent for a perfect night's sleep.

The Trek never went into production. How very surprising.

Perhaps proving that the Japanese car industry can innovate just as well as it once used to imitate, the Daihatsu Trek could have been the answer for every child of the wild, if only it had gone into production.

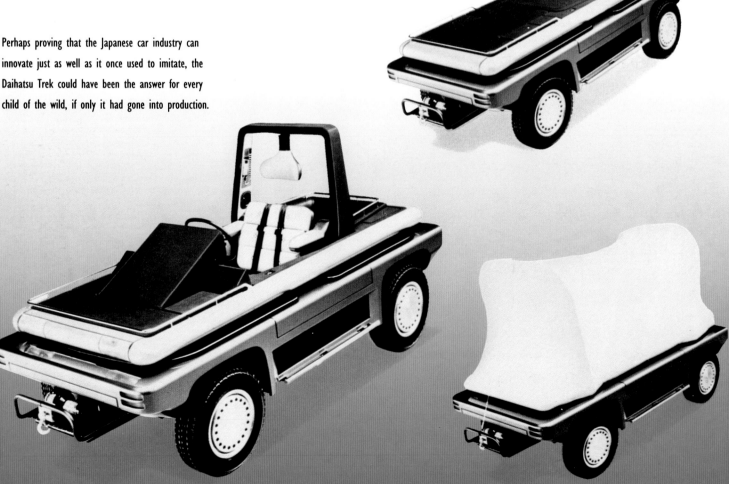

Daimler Silver Flash

SIR BERNARD and Lady Docker were the self-styled King and Queen of Daimler in the 1950s. Although he was boss of the parent company BSA, it was the influence and cash of his railway-rolling-stock tycoon father that propelled him to the top.

She had grown up above a Derby butcher's shop but managed to be widowed by two millionaires by the time she wed Sir Bernard.

Each year at the Motor Show from 1950 to '55, the Dockers ensured that Daimler was the centre of tabloid attention with a show-stopping special car – 'concept cars' as we know them today.

The first had gold-plated fittings, 1952's car sported lizardskin seats and double-glazing, a body covered with tiny, hand-painted stars graced 1954's effort, while 1955 saw the 'Golden Zebra', for which several unfortunate animals of that ilk were slain for the interior trim.

These Docker pet projects attracted publicity, but were so enormously costly to put together that Sir Bernard was eventually booted off the Daimler board for his excessive spending, taking his pushy wife with him. In characteristic style, the first thing they did when 'free' was buy a Rolls-Royce each!

'Silver Flash' shown here was the 1953 show car. Smaller than the other cars in the series (based on the Daimler Regency rather than the straight-eight models), it was just as opulent, with solid-silver hairbrushes and propelling pencils built into the interior trim and fitted red crocodile-skin luggage.

'It was just as opulent, with solid-silver hairbrushes and propelling pencils built into the interior trim.'

It did, though, make a stab at being technically advanced, with its lightweight aluminium body, aerodynamic front, and tinted glass sunroof.

The car recently surfaced after many years in obscurity at an American auction.

How the one-off Daimler Regency 'Silver Flash' looks today after years of exile in an American collection.

Datsun 120Y Coupé

IN 1973, one in 20 new cars sold in the UK was a Datsun. The British motor industry was, understandably, alarmed. People could make all the jokes they liked about yellow peril, and how the 'Made in Japan' label was a euphemism for tin-pot. But, when it came to Japanese cars like Datsuns, the British public couldn't get enough.

'It wasn't a car to drive quickly despite its sporty moniker.'

Keith Hopkins, managing director of British Leyland's Austin Morris division in the early 1970s, recalls that Japanese cars had three things on their side – they were reliable, available, and everything came as standard.

'These were cars that had a radio, when even a heater was extra on an Austin,' he recalls.

Squadrons of cars like this Datsun Sunny 120Y coupé, ugly, plasticky and cramped though they were, purred out of the showroom. It wasn't a car to drive quickly despite its sporty moniker – the 120Y's road manners were dire. However, it started every morning and nothing fell off. 'The Japanese thought that was what

The 120Y coupé, above and left, was hardly a thrill to drive or admire but, for everyday reliability, it was tops.

mattered', says Hopkins. 'And they were right, of course.'

In its four-year career, the 120Y notched up 2.3 million sales around the world. To put that into perspective, it outsold rivals like the Austin Allegro (made for 10 years), Morris Marina (nine years) and Vauxhall Viva HC (nine years) combined.

The British motor industry never quite recovered. But the popularity of cars like the 120Y was instrumental in bringing Nissan's factory to Sunderland.

De Tomaso Deauville

ALEJANDRO DE Tomaso is today a poorly man. Aged 68 and wheelchair-bound, he's recovering from a major brain haemorrhage. Born in Buenos Aires, Argentina, de Tomaso is one of the motor industry's most colourful characters – a hero to some, a scourge to most. His temper is almost as legendary as his deal-making and audacity.

'Advertising tycoons Maurice and Charles Saatchi were enthusiastic owners.'

De Tomaso's most famous car is the Pantera, a mid-engined slingshot that looked set for widespread success in the United States until it was dropped unceremoniously by its sponsor Ford. But he's also, at one time or another, owned Maserati, Innocenti, coachbuilder Ghia and legendary Italian motorbike makers Moto Guzzi and Benelli.

As well as the Pantera, de Tomaso built the Longchamp – a kind of Italian Mercedes SL – and the Deauville you see here, a large saloon looking so like a Jaguar XJ6 you may wonder how Alejandro ever avoided a lawsuit. Both used Ford Mustang engines and components; early Deauvilles, while sumptuously trimmed in soft Italian leathers and suedes, sported hideous plasticky steering wheels straight from a 1970s Ford gas-guzzler.

Prickly and determined he might be, but de Tomaso's car-making never hit the big time. Only a few hundred Deauvilles were made between 1970 and 1988. Among other notables, advertising tycoons Maurice and Charles Saatchi were enthusiastic owners.

Today, de Tomaso – who bought a smart hotel to live in because his American-born wife allegedly hates cooking – is planning his comeback with the Bigua sports car. Like the Deauville, de Tomaso continues to be somewhat of an unknown quantity.

The Deauville's sleek lines pay homage to Jaguar, but its interior clearly shows Ford 'parts bin' influences.

Electraction Rickshaw

'Electraction seems never to have sold any cars at all.'

ONE HUNDRED and eight: the production record for any British electric car. But, even then, it hardly represents real 'sales': the vast majority of the Enfield 8000 electric cars manufactured in 1976 or thereabouts were ordered by the country's regional electricity boards for evaluation and publicity purposes.

One group of Essex entrepreneurs, however, got closer than most to putting Britain on the battery-powered map. Electraction, led by an ex-Ford designer called Roy Haynes, bombarded motor shows in London and Chicago with designs for a two-door saloon, a two-seater roadster, a van and a pick-up featuring hefty packs of heavy-duty Oldham lead acid batteries and a 7.5bhp electric motor.

The strange Rickshaw was the fifth variant. Like the others, it used a mixture of Vauxhall parts and glass fibre It was aimed at sun-drenched holiday resorts or similar 'contained environments' where its 88km (55-mile) range and 48km/h (30mph) top speed would be ideal.

And if the beating of the sun's rays became too much, the fringed 'Surrey' top at the back could be raised as a handy automotive parasol.

'Electraction's marketing director', said the company in 1977, 'has the job of holding back the avalanche of potential customers until production gets underway.' Fond words! Alas, despite relentless promotion, support from the British Trade Development Office, and a merger with famous sports car firm AC, Electraction seems never to have sold any cars at all – like so many other British electric car hopefuls, dashed by the market's total indifference to the concept of plug-in motoring.

The prototype Rickshaw ended up abandoned head-first in an overgrown ditch in Thames Ditton, Surrey, from where it was rescued by a local collector.

Sunshine special: the Electraction Rickshaw could have been a regular sight from Bognor to the Bahamas.

Ellipsis

YOU HAVE to admire Philippe Charbonneaux, aged in his mid-80s and a French industrial designer of some standing, because, to many, his Ellipsis was the laughing stock of the Paris Motor Show in 1992. Yet the thinking behind his diamond-wheel-pattern runabout, with both front and rear steered wheels, was earnest enough.

Thankfully, for students of the truly barmy, the car industry still throws up confections like M. Charbonneaux's diamond-wheel Ellipsis. Said to feature a Volkswagen Beetle engine sited right in the middle, the Ellipsis has yet, however, to be demonstrated in public.

It could allegedly perform a U-turn in a space barely twice its length, and the provision of front and rear steered wheels enabled it to wriggle into the tightest of Parisian parking spaces.

Its long contours with a softly rounded 'point' at either end meant, claimed Charbonneaux, that the car was much safer in accidents, deflecting pedestrians rather than ploughing into them, and 'sliding' away from most potential impacts.

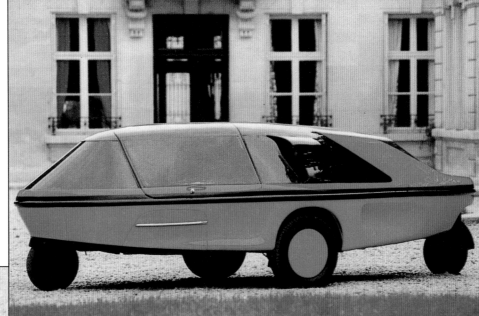

Apparently, there was a Volkswagen Beetle engine powering the two central wheels but Charbonneaux's claims and theories were never independently tested. The whole car appeared to be nothing more than a light plastic model – it was rolled breezily on to its show display by a workman – and the windows were conspicuously, and heavily, tinted, so it was impossible to see how on earth the Ellipsis actually worked . . .

'The whole car appeared to be nothing more than a light plastic model.'

Fairthorpe Atomota

A IR VICE-Marshal Donald Bennett was a remarkable man. His Bomber Command exploits during the Second World War, which earned him his 'Pathfinder' nickname, are legendary. He also pioneered the North Atlantic ferry service – delivering new bombers to Britain – and famously walked across Norway and Sweden when he was shot down after attacking the German battleship *Tirpitz*.

'His hideous-looking Fairthorpe Atom was quite speedy and very thrifty indeed.'

In peacetime, he was a frontrunner in the Berlin airlift (a joint US-British initiative to counter the Soviet blockade of Berlin), and from 1946 to '48 he ran British South American Airways. He also flirted with Liberal politics and, in philanthropic mood, in 1954 formed Fairthorpe after deciding to build the economy car that every austerity-weary British motorist longed for.

With a 250cc BSA motorbike engine at the back and lightweight plastic body, his hideous-looking Fairthorpe Atom was quite speedy and very thrifty indeed, but had no more creature comforts than a tough-as-nails bomber pilot might require. The British motoring public preferred the more seemly Austin A30.

The Atomota was a later version with 650cc BSA or optional Triumph Herald engine and tiny fins grafted on to its sloping rump for a semblance of normality. Only a handful of both Atoms and Atomotas was sold. Bennett, who died in 1986, had more luck with a later series of Fairthorpe sports cars.

'Pathfinder' Bennett's vision of the perfect economy car.

Ford Cortina Mk I Super Estate

'The British public remained singularly unimpressed.'

THE FORD Cortina was planned, from day one, as a best-seller. Pretty simple, light-ish, fairly rapid, quite economical, reasonably roomy, not that expensive, the Cortina ruled the sales chart for almost 20 years because it was just what a sizeable majority of British drivers wanted. In four different guises, the car sold millions and was the standard issue for travelling salesmen for two decades.

If you've got a set of these wood-effect 'Di-Noc' panels wrapped in tissue paper in your loft, Ford Cortina Super Estate (below) owners will want to get to know you!

One of the few blots on the Cortina's otherwise exemplary copybook came about very early on, in fact, when Ford tried its hand at gilding its lily.

Alongside the original Ford Consul Cortina saloons announced in 1962 was a five-door estate. Next to the bigger (1500cc) engined Super models a year later was the Super estate – only, this time, it was richly embellished with polished mahogany side and tailgate panels framed in strips of seasoned pine.

Closer inspection, however, revealed that the panels were made of thin plastic 'Di-Noc' appliqué and that the wooden frame was made of glass fibre.

Such ersatz plankwork was *de rigueur* on US 'station wagons' of the period, helping them blend seamlessly into tree-lined suburban America. But the British public remained singularly unimpressed. Most Cortina Super estate buyers chose two-tone paint instead and the 'woody' option was soon dropped.

Loathed they may have been then, but find an unused set of Di-Noc trim parts now, and you're sitting on, er, plastic gold-dust: such is their rarity, today's Cortina aficionados will trample over each other to buy them.

Ford Consul Classic

IN 1961, the Ford Consul Classic was cool, really cool. Here was a car that, while it was no bigger than your dad's boring, old, sit-up-and-beg car, had all the styling fads and fashionable accessories that you saw on American cars at the pictures.

Big fins at the back, four headlamps at the front under neat little hoods, two-tone paint, whitewall tyres, five chrome stars in the grille and that trendy, reverse-rake rear window shape.

There were even front disc brakes – novel then – a floor-mounted gearlever (wow) and a brand new, five-bearing 1340cc engine.

So, how come the Classic never really caught on?

The problem, apart from the fact that it was heavy and not particularly nice to drive, was those very looks themselves. What had seemed fashionable when it was being designed looked over-styled and ugly next to simple new cars like the Austin 1100. The styling was an over-reaction to the dying days of outrageous cars like the 1959 Cadillac Eldorado Seville with its towering rear fins and larded-on chrome; but on a Dagenham, Essex scale.

The Consul Classic sold poorly for three years before the Cortina's huge success rendered its memory a rare blot on Ford's customer-led copy book.

It might have looked good in the design studio (below) but when the Ford Consul Classic was released in 1961 (right), it was already past its fashion sell-by date. Ford quickly replaced it with the Cortina.

> *'What had seemed fashionable when it was being designed looked over-styled and ugly next to simple new cars.'*

Ford Saxon

'But Ford still tried to conjure up something dashing for the men of Essex.'

THE 1969 Ford Capri was billed in its advertisements and TV commercials as 'The car you always promised yourself'. It was the height of sporty, medallion-man trendiness. But the very first Capri or, more formally, the Ford Consul Capri, was a car customers vowed secretly not to buy.

It was slow, over-engineered and dripping with automotive Americanisms like stylized tail fins, twin headlights and whitewall tyres. The buying public realized that the 1961 Capri was a very lame attempt at a desirable 'personal coupé'. It was subsequently dropped after just three, short years.

But Ford still tried to conjure up something dashing for the men of Essex. And this was it – Saxon, circa 1963.

Devoted car spotters will instantly recognize the 'CND-style' rear lights of the Mk I Cortina, on which Saxon was heavily based. Even the scallop running along the car's flanks from the nose to the neatly cut-off tail is Cortina-like, although the hardtop is totally new.

As with many 'styling exercises', Saxon is different on either side – you can just see the alternative side window treatment on the other side.

Saxon was widely scrutinized and deliberated upon from all angles by regiments of Ford's marketing brains. Their reaction, though, was a resounding thumbs-down. It was to be another six years before the car that flash drivers longed for finally arrived.

Those 'CND' rear lights are tantalizingly familiar – from the Mk I Cortina – but the snappy-looking Saxon never made it past the mock-up stage. Was this a pity?

Ghia Daimler Regency

'Daimler executives didn't know whether to be impressed or disgusted.'

NOW THE Swiss, good though they are at banking, making chocolate and cuckoo clocks, and summits, are not noted as car designers, Unlike us British, you know. Er, except that, in the 1950s, big British cars looked more like the village hall on wheels than serious items of desire.

No production Daimler ever looked as swish as this unique, Ghia-bodied Regency coupé. Alas, Daimler's management was far too toffee-nosed to consider offering it to the public.

The 3.5-litre Daimler Regency typified them: cumbersome, over-engineered and, in appearance, something between a submarine and a public school matron.

It was this unlikely object that a little-known Swiss offshoot of the famous Italian Ghia design company used as a basis for a design transformation. They stripped away the crinoline and bustle and slipped the Daimler chassis into a slinky cocktail dress. The picture shows the blue

and beige car just days after it was completed, taking a rest while on its way to the March 1955 Geneva Motor Show.

Daimler executives didn't know whether to be impressed or disgusted as they swarmed all over this 'two/four seater hardtop coupé'. The company was used to building sombre limousines and probably regarded a car like this as rather too nouveau for its image – too much like a Jaguar. Furthermore, a king's

ransom price of £3250 was quoted for further handmade replicas.

Daimler was in those days car maker to the Royal Family – preferred even to Rolls-Royce. Alas, its stick-in-the-mud policy – the company could not countenance putting a Swiss-designed car, no matter how sleek, into production – eventually forced it into enemy hands. Jaguar took over in 1960, and Daimler's individuality quickly evaporated.

Hanomag

'Hanomag had now reached the limit to which people would descend in the name of economy.'

THE GERMAN Hanomag is probably the only wicker-bodied car ever to go into series production. Hanomag was an old-established maker of railway locomotives in Hanover when, in 1924, it took a branch line into the car world. Unlike its mainstay products, though, Hanomag cars were tiny.

With a single-cylinder, water-cooled, 500cc engine at the back, narrow track, a single front headlight, and seating for only two, the Hanomag was evidently one for the common people. In four years, almost 16,000 were bought by them. It was the ideal vehicle for steep, narrow country roads and earned the nickname *Kommissbrot* – meaning 'army loaf' – because of its perpendicular shape and rounded ends.

Hanomag Kommissbrot (below) and raffia relative (right).

The open-topped basketweave version was aimed at the motorist hampered by an even smaller bank balance, and did without such niceties as a windscreen. A few hundred were reputedly sold, but Hanomag had now reached the limit to which people would descend in the name of economy. The rear engine already made handling a Hanomag tricky; the featherlight raffia body made it so light that a gentle breeze would blow it off course.

Survivors are rare. This one, owned by Martin Wolf, is still going strong, though – managing a creditable 14 steep, uphill kilometres (9 miles) in 35 minutes on a Swiss hillclimb three years ago.

Hudson Commodore

HUDSON, FOUNDED in 1909, was among the last of the American 'independents' – car makers who struggled and ultimately failed in the face of competition from industry giants, such as the mighty Ford, General Motors and Chrysler.

Although its cars during the 1920s and '30s were pretty unremarkable – with the exception of those with its technically advanced 'Electric Hand' automatic gearbox – Hudson shocked the burghers of Detroit in 1948 with its new range of 'Step Down' cars.

Not only were they sleek and handsome, but their unitary construction featured rear wheels mounted actually

The Commodore sedan sat at the head of Hudson's range of advanced and glamorous 'Step Down' cars.

inside the chassis frame. There was also independent front suspension.

The range began with the budget-priced Pacemaker and worked its way up through the Super Six, Hornet and Wasp to the opulent Commodore, shown here, with Hudson's traditional 4.2-litre straight-eight. A brand new 5-litre straight-six cylinder engine introduced in 1951 for the Hornet boasted 145bhp and made the car a force to be reckoned with in American stock-car racing.

For sheer 1950s American glamour, a

'For sheer glamour a Hudson Super Wasp Hollywood hardtop coupé was hard to beat.'

Hudson Super Wasp Hollywood hardtop coupé was hard to beat.

Over 145,000 Hudsons were sold in 1950 but the 'Big Three' majors took no hostages when it came to stiff competition. In 1954 Hudson merged with Nash to form American Motors, and by 1957 the venerable Hudson marque was dead.

Hyundai Pony

'It's not exactly a vehicle you'd cross the road to drool over.'

IF YOU'VE bought a Korean-made Daewoo, and the company tells us an amazing number of British people already have, chances are that you're pretty happy with it. In fact, if you are not we'd like to hear from you, because its bubble of self-confidence is getting more prickable by the, er, Daewoo.

It's certainly no pulse-racer but the Hyundai Pony (below) introduced the world to a new breed of car, the Korean one, when it was launched in 1974.

It's just over 20 years ago, after all, that Korea made its first car and here it is, the Hyundai Pony. It's not exactly a vehicle you'd cross the road to drool over.

It possesses the visual charm of a tinny mid-1970s Datsun crossed with a Morris Marina – although the styling, amazingly, was by that usually inspired Italian, Giorgio Giugiaro. Engines and

other mechanical bits were provided by Mitsubishi, while most of the expertise and know-how involved in building the factory and showing Koreans how to actually make cars came from Britain, orchestrated by an ex-British Leyland executive called George Turnbull.

His colleagues in the West Midlands might have jeered when he headed east,

but just look at what Turnbull started. Hyundai, Daewoo, Ssangyong, Kia and now electronics giant Samsung are a new massed rank with a respectable position in the world car industry hierarchy.

Scoff at the old Hyundai you may do but the Koreans, although recently suffering from abysmal labour relations, could soon have the last laugh.

Innocenti Regent

IF YOU think you recognize the infamous Austin Allegro, think again: this is the super-rare Italian version. Not just sold there – built there too. Yes, Austin went all sophisticated with a local Latin version in 1974 in a desperate attempt to shore up its crumbling Continental empire. You see, at the time British Leyland had all the makings of a pan-European company like Ford or General Motors. It built cars in Spain, Belgium and at its Innocenti plant in Italy.

'It sold so badly that it was dropped after just one year.'

Minis and Austin 1100/1300s had been the staple product until this car, the Innocenti Regent 1300 De Luxe, was launched. You can tell it from a normal Allegro because of the fancy wheels and badges, and the separate, opening front quarterlight windows to help ventilation on those baking Italian autostradas.

Mamma's Regent also got a round steering wheel, instead of the bizarre 'quartic' one on English Matron's.

It sold so badly that it was dropped after just one year and Innocenti was plunged into receivership. Other than that, of course, a splendid machine and one that no self-respecting Allegro collector can be satisfied without . . .

Innocenti turned from making the BMC 1100 (right) to the Allegro (below), with disastrous results.

Invicta Black Prince

WHEN THE end of the Second World War came, it brought with it a flurry of British attempts to cash in on the huge, pent-up demand for new cars. Some, like Healey and Bristol, went on to greatness. The Invicta Black Prince, however, was too clever for its own good.

An enormous luxury car, it featured a Meadows six-cylinder, 3-litre engine with two spark plugs per cylinder, and power was transmitted through a complex version of today's constantly variable automatic transmission. Called a 'Brockhouse Hydro-Kinetic Turbo Transmitter', this device did away with a conventional gearbox altogether.

Other unusual refinements included electrically powered jacks, 24-volt starter, even a trickle-fed heater for the radiator.

The car's individual, handmade bodywork was elegant and sumptuous but, at almost £4000 by 1949, a Black Prince set you back around ten times the cost of a typical small family saloon like a Ford Popular – well beyond the means of even the most successful 1940s black marketeers. And the transmission reputedly rendered the car, of which 16 were finally made between 1946 and 1950 in Virginia Water, Surrey, almost impossible to reverse!

> *'The car's individual, handmade bodywork was elegant and sumptuous.'*

The Black Prince was elegant (bottom) and expensive but ambitious mechanical parts (below) let it down.

Isotta-Fraschini Monterosa

'It was an enormous luxury car with a 3.4-litre V8 engine mounted at the back.'

T HE ISOTTA-Fraschini marque has a history of short bursts of glory. Founded in 1900, in the early part of the century it was Italy's second largest car maker after Fiat, making a range of sporting, aristocratic machines and high-speed tourers.

After the First World War it based all its designs around a fabulous straight-eight engine and its products established themselves as some of the most expensive and exclusive cars in Europe. But car-making petered out in 1936 as the company concentrated on its other speciality, the construction of ship and aero engines.

The Tipo 8C Monterosa of 1947 was an attempt to restart car-making activities. It was an enormous luxury car with a 3.4-litre V8 engine mounted at the back, and the first few built had their cross-shaped chassis clothed in dramatic fashion by some of Italy's finest coachbuilders, such as Zagato and Touring. This aerodynamic convertible belies its near-50-year age and it was designed by Boneschi – still in business today making truck bodies.

But the Italian state, by then in control, decreed that Isotta-Fraschini must stick to making industrial engines, and it shut the fledgling Monterosa

In 1946, the Monterosa was the epitome of high-tech, with its rear-mounted V8 engine and exotic coachwork. Problem was, the Italian government didn't approve.

project down unceremoniously after a year when just 20 had been built.

Large Isotta-Fraschini power units have continued to be made to this day. However, ambitious plans have recently been announced to relaunch Isotta cars in collaboration with Audi. The new T8 roadster is currently under development.

Jaguar XKSS

'Nine gutted XKSSs were still smouldering in the cold light of that February morning.'

THE NIGHT of 12 February 1957 started normally enough at Jaguar's Coventry factory. The last workers cycled home through the gates of the Browns Lane plant; the nightwatchman settled down with the local paper for what he imagined would be an uneventful shift.

But, by morning, a raging inferno had ripped through the Browns Lane works, scorching its way through everything in its path. Around 270 cars were destroyed, among them the few existing examples of the scintillating new XKSS sports car.

Launched just weeks before the blaze, the XKSS looked pretty much like the Le Mans-winning Jaguar D-Type. Not surprisingly, really, as it was merely a roadgoing version of the racer with decent seats, wind-up windows, bumpers and a hood. Jaguar had withdrawn from

The XKSS (right and opposite), being a road version of the D-Type racer, was killed in Jaguar's catastrophic 1957 fire, rendering brochure imagery (below) obsolete.

competition and this was its novel ruse to use up unsold D-Type structures and, perhaps, put the XKSS into production as a proper sports car.

Nine gutted XKSSs were still smouldering in the cold light of that February morning; some had literally melted away as their aluminium bodywork was consumed by the intense heat. Only 16 reached customers and, as Jaguar poured its all into rebuilding the factory, the 250bhp XKSS was put on the backburner – forever.

Jeep Jeepster

'The Jeepster nevertheless lasted only three years before Jeep decided to can it.'

EVEN THE makers of all the macho new four-wheel-drive off-roaders that are so heavily promoted nowadays acknowledge that the vast majority of them will never leave tarmac and genuinely take to rough terrain. They know that they will spend their days ambling through suburbia, between home, school and shopping mall.

The extra components and strengthening needed to allow a 4x4 to cope with the rigours of the rough make them slower and thirstier than they need to be. But no marketing man in his right mind would consider advertising a two-wheel-drive Shogun, Discovery or Vitara.

However, in 1948, Willys Jeep was anxious to find new markets for its vehicles after the Second World War and decided to offer the Jeepster as a 'sports phaeton' – in other words, a nifty-looking convertible – with all the rugged charm of the normal Jeep but none of its clanking, terra-defying hardware.

Coveted today as one of post-war America's most characterful cruising machines, the Jeepster nevertheless lasted only three years before Jeep decided to can it and concentrate on its four-wheel-drive products. In those days, however, this decision was not taken for fickle marketing reasons: rather a world slowly recovering from the ravages of war needed every off-roader Jeep – and soon Land-Rover – could make.

Jeep's Jeepster looked the part of the sporty leisure car but did without the four-wheel-drive paraphernalia. It's now a rare and desirable gem on the US old car scene.

Lancia Beta Coupé Hi-Fi

'The Hi-Fi did little to halt Lancia's disastrous sales slump.'

IN THE late 1970s, Lancias had quite a reputation in Britain – a reputation for rusting, that is. Tales of engines breaking off corroded mountings, and brand new paintwork soon deeply pitted by telltale brown marks were legion at the time.

Lancia hoped that a decent stereo, fancy wheels and a huge rear spoiler on the Beta Coupé could salvage its rusty reputation in the UK. Aston Martin did the spruce-up but the Hi-Fi failed to stop terminally falling sales.

Once seen as an Italian version of BMW much favoured by the chic middle classes, regrettably Lancias turned into undesirable backstreet bangers when just a couple of years old. In 1993 the marque disappeared from Britain altogether after all efforts to market it here had failed.

The Beta Coupé Hi-Fi was born in the eye of this disastrous public relations storm. In 1981 rows of unsold Beta Coupés stood on windswept English airfields so the importer asked Aston Martin Tickford to help shift them.

Aston kitted 300 out with alloy wheels and low-profile tyres, a rear spoiler and front air-dam, and snazzy side stripes. And, of course, a decent hi-fi – a Voxson Indianapolis unit with graphic equaliser, four speakers and an electric aerial. No CD autochanger, this, but smart for the early 1980s.

Unfortunately, though, the damage was done and the Hi-Fi did little to halt Lancia's disastrous sales slump. Still, the stereo did at least help drown out the usual Beta squeaks and rattles.

Lea-Francis Lynx

'THE PULSATING car of the moment – and of the future' ran the advert in 1960. Never was an advertising slogan so misplaced. With car manufacture fizzled out by the late 1950s, the old-established Lea-Francis company, whose Coventry roots went back to the dawn of the bicycle era, was losing money hand over fist when its biggest shareholder stepped in as chairman.

'Benfield wanted two cigars in a catamaran with a round radiator.'

A building contractor, Kenneth Benfield knew zilch about making cars. But he certainly knew what he liked.

He'd seen magazine pictures of the latest Italian supercars and, thus inspired, he ordered his staff to cobble together a snazzy sports car to revive Lea-Francis, using a Ford Zephyr six-cylinder engine for power.

The firm's PR man, also a part-time cartoonist and stand-up comedian, was drafted in as unwilling stylist. 'Benfield wanted two cigars in a catamaran with a round radiator,' recalled one insider.

To make it appear even more up-to-the-minute, the 1960 'Lynx' Motor Show car was painted a vivid lilac with gold-plated trim. But the catchy ads, and a cover appearance on *Vanity Fair*, couldn't stem the showgoers' scornful laughter at the sight of the £2096 monster.

Lea-Francis was so hard up it couldn't afford to make any cars after the three prototypes until they were ordered. And as none were, the Lynx sloped off quietly into obscurity.

Below: 'Havana' shape clearly visible in profile of Lynx.

Lincoln Continental Mk IV

IT'S UNLIKELY we'll ever see cars as gratuitously enormous as the 1959 Cadillac Eldorado Seville again. As much a late 20th century American icon as Warhol's soup tin, the '59 Caddy took the annual Detroit model change fad to its longest, widest, glitziest, most be-finned limits. You know the car – Danny De Vito drove one in *Tin Men*, Natalie Cole had a hit tune about a pink one, and they've appeared in a thousand airbrushed Athena posters.

> *'A car less 'continental' would be hard to imagine.'*

Doing the Continental: Lincoln on display at Turin, '58.

But who recalls its bitterest rival?

The 1959 Lincoln Continental, at over 5790mm (19ft) long and weighing a gargantuan 2216kg (4880lb), was just as gross. Indeed, Lincoln, Ford's luxury car subsidiary, billed it as 'longer, lower, wider' than any previous model. Its 7047cc V8 engine was similarly elephantine.

The styling, although devoid of the space rocket fins of the Cadillac, was as outrageous in its own way, boasting the chrome of a dozen Morris Minors, four 'narrowed eye' headlamps and a dashboard like a jukebox.

Its reverse-slope rear window inspired that on Britain's own Ford Anglia but there the comparison with European cars stopped. This one was shown at the 1958 Turin Motor Show, but a car less 'continental' would be hard to imagine.

Perhaps it was tainted by association with the Edsel, Ford's other 1958 debutante and a legendary sales fiasco.

Maybe the larger-than-life(less) Continental just never possessed the Cadillac's Elvis-like charisma.

But significantly the 1961 Continental that replaced it was one of the least-adorned, albeit still aircraft carrier-sized, cars America has ever produced.

Lloyd 650

'Fuel consumption was a miserly 18km/litre (50mpg).'

COD IS probably Grimsby's lasting gift to civilization, not cars. But the Lincolnshire fishing town's unparalleled four-wheeled contribution to motoring's hall of fame, the Lloyd 650 of 1946, was in fact a technological masterpiece. Its only other car, pre-war, was an unremarkable 350cc midget.

Here's the prototype of the technologically advanced Lloyd 650 on test near Grimsby in 1946. The high cost of making it meant the car would never be a success.

The German DKW F2 of 1933 was the first affordable production car ever to combine front-wheel drive with the compactness of an engine mounted transversely at the front. But the lilliputian Lloyd was the first British attempt to exploit the same technology, beating the Mini by 13 years.

The 650 was devised by a local Grimsby engineer and garage proprietor,

F. Roland Lloyd, to sate the post-war appetite for new cars.

Virtually every part was Grimsby-made: the aluminium twin-cylinder engine with ingenious double-acting oil pump, gearbox, chassis, body – even wheels and brakes. Rack-and-pinion steering made the car easy to handle, and fuel consumption was a miserly 18km/litre (50mpg).

But this determinedly local enterprise – the 650 was launched at a trade fair in the 'Wonderland' amusement park at the nearby seaside resort of Cleethorpes – could obviously never topple industry giants Ford and Austin.

Fewer than 400 four-seater convertible 650s were made until the car's demise in 1952, when Grimsby returned to trawling more familiar waters, battered but wiser.

Lotus Eminence

INDUSTRIAL ESPIONAGE is one of the curses of the automobile industry Car manufacturers usually keep their future plans closely guarded secrets, fearful that intelligence about new models will only help their rivals to outsmart them. But not Lotus.

In 1985, it informed the world of its advance strategy for the ultimate limousine, the Eminence, which was to out-Cadillac Cadillac. It issued detailed comparisons with heavyweight competitors like the Rolls-Royce Phantom, Mercedes-Benz 500SEL and Caddy Fleetwood, even down to respective wheel sizes.

Eminence would catapult its six passengers to 97km/h (60mph) in under 6 seconds and then on to a maximum speed of 257km/h (160mph), all in V8-powered, four-wheel-drive, anti-lock braked, armour-plated opulence.

'. . . A high technology Premier Limousine . . . total control in extreme manoeuvres . . . secure, self-contained luxury' boasted the blurb – stuff apparently to make wicked dictators and Hollywood moguls jam Lotus's Norfolk switchboard with orders.

But two years later General Motors had taken over, and all smart-ass talk about unseating Cadillac as the world's

'All smart-ass talk about unseating Cadillac as the world's premier top-people's car was banned.'

premier top-people's car was banned. Only this drawing remains, by Harris Mann, stylist of the Austin Allegro, as a reminder of what a British Prime Minister might now be whisked off to Chequers in.

Harris Mann's drawing of a potential Lotus limousine.

Lotus Eminence

'Driverless' Mercedes

THE 'DRIVERLESS' car has been something of a 'Holy Grail' quest for engineers for many years: relaxing in your personalized cocoon while neither driving nor employing a chauffeur is a concept that's kept many a boffin awake at night.

'The car never left the traffic-free confines of Continental's test track.'

German tyremaker Continental, though, actually pioneered one such creation back in 1968, an outwardly normal Mercedes saloon with a boot packed full of computer equipment.

With a controller in a tower supervizing at the company's 'Contidrome' test track in Germany, the automatic Mercedes could spend many a contented day bowling round and round the circuit, its two measuring coils mounted on the front bumper reading the magnetic field generated by a cable embedded in the circuit's concrete surface.

When it sensed that the car was veering alarmingly off-course, on a bend or in a sidewind, an electric message transmitted to the wheel corrected the steering, as if some unseen ghost was at the helm.

Magnetic cable buried in concrete (above) helped Continental's special Mercedes (left) to drive itself.

The car never left the traffic-free confines of Continental's test track, though, where it dutifully trundled round all day without needing periodic stops for coffee and cigarettes like most test drivers. Indeed, no-one has since properly developed the idea of a hands-free car for the public highway. When it comes to unmanned passenger-carrying vehicles, London's Docklands Light Railway is still about as close as you can get.

Michelotti Triumph TR3

'Webster's attempts to discover where the car was being made were fruitless.'

BROTHERS RAYMOND, Derek and Neville Flower fancied themselves as motor industry operators. Captain Raymond had initiated an abortive venture to produce an Egyptian racing car, the Phoenix, that competed in the official national racing colour of purple, and with Neville he also steered the Frisky bubble car into production. Derek was the financial wizard.

In the 1950s they had grand plans to make their own sports cars too, using the Triumph TR3 chassis. But the company's engineering chief Harry Webster was wary of supplying them . . . especially as they claimed that an up-to-the-minute prototype could be built in a mere three months. The Flowers, however, were shrinking violets when it came to revealing exactly how this would be done.

With curiosity aroused, Webster gave them one TR3 chassis and challenged them to prove their claim. Within 10 days he'd chosen the most complex of a sheaf of artfully-executed proposal drawings the brothers presented to him. But Webster's attempts to discover where the car was being made were fruitless: he had to bide his time.

Less than three months later the striking two-seater you see here was delivered to the Triumph works. 'It was beautifully made, exquisitely trimmed and a runner', remembers Webster.

A hearty lunch with the delivery driver eventually elicited the fact that the car came from Italy, specifically from the drawing board of one Giovanni Michelotti.

It proved to be the inspiration for the Triumph Herald and sparked a 10-year relationship between Michelotti and Triumph that resulted in such classic cars as the TR4, Spitfire, GT6, 2000, Dolomite and Stag.

The Flower brothers never did get that deal, but all three prospered and survive today.

Wild styling was foretaste of impending Triumph Herald.

Miele

A MIELE WASHING machine or dishwasher is a must-have for every smart kitchen. Expensive jeans from Cannes to Chester wouldn't be caught spinning in anything less. But in 1912 the German founders of Miele, Carl Miele and Reinhard Zinkann, were convinced they could also make the king of cars.

'After 125 cars had been built in two years Miele decided its future lay with the household appliances.'

Introduced in 1912, the Miele K1 tourer boasted a 17bhp four-cylinder engine. German car magazine *Stahlrad und Automobil* said: 'No other automobile factory has achieved the same success in such a short time as Miele'. A bigger 22bhp K2 model soon joined it, together with a long-wheelbase limousine said to cost what the mayor of Guetersloh, Miele's home town, earned in a year.

They were exported as far afield as Brazil and Russia, but after 125 cars had been built in two years Miele decided its future lay with the household appliances built alongside the car production line.

Above: Dr Zinkann and Herr Miele in their newly discovered car. Left: How it looked back in 1912.

It was long assumed that all examples of Miele cars had disappeared into the mists of time. But Rudolph Miele and Peter Zinkann, the descendants of the founders who still own the private firm, nevertheless yearned to find one. A remarkably original survivor eventually turned up in Norway after a five-year hunt; it had led a hard life as a taxi and a driving-school car but now rubs wheelnuts with early wooden washing machines in Miele's museum.

Minissima

'The Minissima was as long as most cars were wide.'

I N A few short years' time, according to the rumours, we will see an all-new Mini that promises to be as revolutionary and endearing as the original was in 1959. But thoughts have turned to a 'New Mini' many times before. The car's creator Sir Alec Issigonis had a crack at it in the late 1960s, and the Minissima was a promising reinterpretation in 1973.

Stylist William Towns came up with this novel interpretation of the evergreen Mini in 1973, but British Leyland judged it just too radical to produce.

The spartan-lined 'one box' design packed the Mini's venerable A-Series engine and front-wheel drive into a tiny wheelbase. The Minissima was as long as most cars were wide – so short was it, in fact, that it could be parked end-on to the kerb without it protruding dangerously into the street. You could safely disembark straight on to the pavement through the car's only door, which was sited centrally at the back.

The Minissima was the work of the late William Towns, best known for styling the Aston Martin DBS and Lagonda. British Leyland couldn't summon up the imagination to make such a radical runabout but the design eventually bore fruit for Towns: a bicycle maker called Elswick renamed it the 'Envoy', widened the rear door and found a niche for the Minissima – as a car into which the wheelchair-bound driver could easily manoeuvre and instantly set off. Even so, few were actually sold.

Morgan Plus Four Plus

'A paltry 26 Plus Four Pluses were sold in three years.'

PICTURE A Morgan and the image that springs to most minds is as English as Yorkshire puddings or red pillar boxes. Wind in the hair, grit in the teeth, and vintage simplicity in all things – from the separate, hand-beaten wings to the outside, boot-mounted, spare wheel and trio of tiny windscreen wipers. Flying goggles are a must.

You don't imagine a stylish two-seater coupé with – gulp – glass fibre bodywork.

But that's just what Morgan dished up to a disbelieving public in 1964 under the name of the Plus Four Plus (crumbs, even the quintessentially British golfing trouser reference was given the '60s treatment). For Morgan, it was radical.

Company boss Peter Morgan was afraid his loyal customers, who'd been buying pretty much the same car since the first four-wheeled Morgan was launched in 1936, would one day desert him for more modish pastures. Hence the pretty new face – albeit on the identical, bone-shaking Morgan chassis.

The Plus Four Plus was Morgan's effort at going modern in 1964. From the front (right) and in side profile (below) it was handsome, although many felt its roof (left, below) looked curious. Buyer preference for the traditional Morgan meant just 26 PFPs were sold.

Quite the opposite happened, in fact, with an immediate upsurge in orders for the classic traditional design that's continued unabated ever since. By contrast, a paltry 26 Plus Four Pluses were sold in three years, and all thoughts of changing the Morgan formula were rapidly forgotten.

Moschino Metro

CARS THESE days take too long to design to pander to fashion; they're too expensive to produce to be fripperies. Which tends to mean that their colours and interior trim err on the side of universal and sober acceptability. Hence the profusion of straightforward reds, blues, silvers and whites, mostly with grey trim, that we all have to put up with.

'Moschino did its bit for Britain by decorating a white Metro in black-painted lucky symbols.'

In 1994, however, the Italian fashion industry set out to prove that not all small cars need to look uniformly standard-issue. At the Turin Motor Show, Italy's world renowned couture houses showed us how.

On the carwalk, Gucci stuck red and green stripes down the side of a Fiat Cinquecento, Fendi added their trademark gold and brown parallel lines to a Suzuki Swift, Krizia kitted a VW Golf estate out with snakeskin-pattern leather, and Missoni swapped Lancia badges on a Y10 for its own logos.

Moschino, though, did its bit for Britain by decorating a white Metro in black-painted lucky symbols – cats, horseshoes and number 13s. Inside the car sported black-and-white striped seat covers with red edging.

The cars were all auctioned after the show, with proceeds going to AIDS research. So, somewhere in Italy, although it looks like a Metro that's been attacked by a graffiti gang, someone is pounding the streets in a Moschino designer original. Perhaps grey with black seats isn't so bad after all.

Moschino's ritzy Metro brought luck for AIDS charities.

Nubar Gulbenkian's London Taxi

'Nubar decided to have a special miniature limousine built.'

N UBAR SARKIS Gulbenkian, monocle in his right eye and orchid always in his buttonhole, was one of London's most recognizable playboys. He lived at the Ritz, whiled away many an hour at the St James Club, married three times, and enjoyed a tycoon's lifestyle.

'Turns on a sixpence', said Nubar, 'whatever that is'.

He was an oil mogul. Like his father before him, the Armenian Jew Calouste Gulbenkian, Nubar had helped to develop the UK's oil interests in the Middle East. Old Calouste's acumen at deal-making meant he owned five per cent of BP's shares which, when passed on to his son, earned Nubar the nickname 'Mr Five Per Cent'; Nubar was no less astute, but spent more time enjoying his vast fortune than dad ever had.

And what did he spend it on? The good life, sure, and cars. At first it was ultra-fast vintage supercars; then a string of specially made and mostly very ugly Rolls-Royces.

But, weary of the usual rich man's playthings, Nubar decided to have a special miniature limousine built – based on London's superbly manoeuvrable taxi. It was carefully constructed in 1965 to his own design by a coachbuilder in Battersea, south London called FLM Panelcraft, and incorporated gold-plated fittings, a glass Lalique bonnet mascot, and a rear end that looked as if a

horsedrawn brougham had simply been welded on to the rump of a black cab. Natural wickerwork panels were attached to the 'carriage' end of the car.

Gulbenkian was mighty proud of it, once famously quoted as saying: 'I understand it can turn on a sixpence – whatever that is'.

It was one of London's most famous cars, but when Gulbenkian died in 1972, aged 72, the one-off taxi went to California. It still exists, making £23,000 at a British auction in 1993.

Ogle Aston Martin

'THIS MUST be just about the most desirable object ever produced by the British motor industry', said Raymond Baxter on BBC1's popular science and technology programme *Tomorrow's World* in 1972. 'It's a beautiful piece of design.'

This was music to the ears of Tom Karen and his team at Ogle Design. After all, ripping the body off an Aston Martin and trying to replace it with an even more dramatic one was never going to be an easy job.

The tobacco company Wills had commissioned Ogle to build a unique car to help launch a new brand of cigarettes called Sotheby. The resulting Aston Martin DBS sports car had a dramatic wedge profile, a raised tail and an all-Triplex Sundym glass roof with built-in heating element and special gold strips to deflect strong sunlight. 'I was quite proud of it', recalls Karen today. 'Until then, no-one else had stuck glass on to the outside of a car to give it a completely glazed effect'.

But its most remarkable feature was two rows of 11 rear lights that worked sequentially: four indicators, two reversing lights and 16 brake lights of which the three nearest the 'corners' of the cars were brighter in illumination to show following vehicles how progressive the braking was. There were also two reflectors. They were a safety aid, says Karen, but also very dramatic visually.

The 'Sotheby Special' was first shown at the 1972 Montreal Motor Show. The bodywork was painted dark blue picked out with gold coachlines – just like the fag packets. The Sotheby cigarettes were a flop, but one other Ogle Aston was

Ogle gave Aston DBS radical rear lights (right) and plenty of light through Triplex Sundym glass (below).

'Its most remarkable feature was two rows of 11 rear lights that worked sequentially.'

ordered by a wealthy Buckinghamshire woman – the claret-coloured car shown here. Both cars have had a succession of owners but happily they both still survive, the original car in Kent.

Ogle SX250

'It was one of the swishest looking new cars at the show.'

I N THE hall of the great and good of the motoring industry, one Boris Porter doesn't figure very prominently. That's not surprising, really: you would not expect the one-time joint-managing director of the Helena Rubinstein Company in Britain to be much of a car name, would you?

A happy Boris Porter takes delivery of the smart new Ogle-bodied Daimler, with violet interior, in 1962.

Yet it was this patrician captain of cosmetics who helped shape a distinctive generation of British sports cars.

Mr Porter had seen a rather trendy coupé exhibited at the 1962 Earl's Court Motor Show styled by industrial designer David Ogle – a man who shot to fame as the design genius behind the good looks of Bush transistor radios. Called the Ogle SX250, the coupé sat on a Daimler SP250 chassis, with 2.5-litre V8 engine, and featured glass fibre bodywork. Not

only that, it was one of the swishest looking new cars at the show – and Boris Porter wanted one.

So he asked Ogle to build him a copy. Only, his car had to be individual.

The interior was finished in a colour that had been specially created for Ms Rubinstein's Knightsbridge flat, 'French Violet', while the bodywork was painted in 'Opalescent Golden Sand'. Other features included a special sunroof, reclining seats and thick carpets.

But why was the car so significant? Well, Ogle Design got a lucrative contract to tackle packaging of seven Rubinstein products, for one thing. But the addition of Mr Porter's personal touches to the smart new Daimler helped to bring the car to the attention of Reliant; the three-wheeler maker eventually bought the rights to the car's design and in 1964 launched it, now with Ford power, as the first Reliant Scimitar. The rest, as they say, is history.

Owen Sedanca

'Inside, it was a cocoon of coffee Dralon and tan suede leather.'

GERALD RONSON has certainly tasted the spice of life and experienced its ups-and-downs – from running property-to-petrol-stations group Heron, one of Britain's biggest privately-owned companies, to doing 'bird' in Ford Open Prison for his part in the Guinness share-support scandal. He's been a car manufacturer too. Well, almost.

Gerald Ronson sponsored the Owen Sedanca but the fuel crisis of the 1970s meant buyers were scarce.

But for the 1974 oil crisis, his Sedanca might now be as common a sight in monied London circles as the Mercedes-Benz SL is. It was inspired by Ronson's own personal car of the time, a Lamborghini Espada, and was intended

to provide sumptuous seating for four passengers in a supremely swish and totally British-made coupé.

The very un-Italian part was the complete Jaguar XJ6 floorpan and purring engine underneath. Inside, it was a cocoon of coffee Dralon and tan suede leather. Hidden in the driver's door was even a silver-backed hairbrush.

But with a price tag of £8500, the Sedanca looked a costly gas-guzzler and all 80 orders that Ronson's smart H.R. Owen showrooms took were cancelled in the wake of the Middle Eastern oil crisis. Two cars, costing tens of thousands of pounds, were eventually made for Arab brothers to use on their Oxfordshire country estate. Ironically, one was sold at auction in October 1994 for just £3740, less than the price of a current Lada.

Panther Rio

'It was essentially a Dolomite stripped of its lowly coachwork and re-clothed in hand-beaten aluminium.'

FOR SOME, a good car is never quite good enough. And the Triumph Dolomite 1850 and Sprint of the late 1970s were good cars. Lots of people thought of them as sort-of British BMWs, although British Leyland's appalling labour relations had a devastating effect on the cars' quality levels.

Fashion designer and replica car maker Robert Jankel was convinced they could be improved, however. He knew the underpinnings and running gear were fine but reckoned that the looks and interior trim were just a little bit, well, common for some tastes.

So he came up with the Panther Rio, which was essentially a Dolomite stripped of its lowly coachwork and re-clothed in hand-beaten aluminium.

The result was supposed to be more elegant, more like a miniature Bentley or Lagonda, while the interior was sumptuously retrimmed in rich leather in keeping with the exterior, with deep carpets and lustrous walnut plastered everywhere.

Only 38 were made. Perhaps people thought the Rio, in its quest to be subtle, looked too anonymous. Or maybe it was simply because the Rio Especiale (with 16-valve Sprint engine) at £8996 cost well over twice what the ordinary Triumph did.

Behind the façade, the Rio was all Triumph Dolomite.

Panther Deville

THE 'REPLICAR' was a peculiar trend that originated in the USA in 1964 when Excalibur and Ruger revealed their beautifully-made copies of the Mercedes-Benz SSK and Blower Bentley respectively, only both of them were powered by modern, untemperamental engines. Perhaps as a reaction to the 'sameness' of then-current car designs, they caught on – particularly for rich violets who weren't too keen on shrinking. Tommy Steele was Britain's best-known Excalibur driver.

'About 60 of these hand-built pimp-mobiles were made until production ended in 1985.'

Britain joined the trend in 1972 with the Panther J72, a Jaguar-powered copy of the 1930s SS 100 Jaguar sports car. The Panther Deville followed in 1974.

Sitting on a giant 361cm (142in) wheelbase, the tubular-framed monster used Jaguar 6- and 12-cylinder engines and was supposed to ape the incredible 1930 Bugatti Royale – a near-legendary car of which just six were built. Real vintage car enthusiasts sneered – especially at the doors of the Deville saloon, which were pinched from a humble Austin 1800 and none-too-artfully melded into the overall design.

About 60 of these handbuilt pimp-mobiles were made until production ended in 1985, including two-door convertibles and this example (right), the last, a pink and gold six-door limousine. Mmm, now that's what I call tasteful . . .

Bugatti-esque Deville (below) shocked purists; last car made (right and below, right) was Las Vegas on wheels.

Peykan

'Making the Peykan Britain's unlikely number one export car.'

AT FIRST, there doesn't seem much to connect the 1979 revolution in Iran with the fate of the average Coventry car worker. But when the Persian Shah was overthrown, many workers at Talbot's Coventry factories lost their Christmas bonuses. Caught in the middle was the Peykan.

You'd have to look long and hard at the cars to spot the difference between a Peykan and a Hillman Hunter. Apart from the grille badge there was none: the Peykan was simply a Hunter whose complete parts were gathered together and carefully packed into crates in Coventry. These were then shipped to the Middle East where the Iran National Industrial Manufacturing Co assembled them into Peykans.

Ever since the days of the Rootes Group in 1969, hundreds of thousands of 'CKD' – standing for 'completely knocked down' – kits had been sold to Iran, frequently making the Peykan Britain's unlikely number one export car.

Although internal strife interrupted deliveries, by 1981 the crates were seaborne once more, and continued to be so until 1987, by which time the Hunter, a simple, rugged beast ideally suited to hostile Iranian roads, was but a distant memory for British drivers.

The Peykan (below) was a Hillman Hunter built in Iran from British parts; this is a proposed styling update.

Pininfarina Bentley T-Series

'The press christened it the most expensive used car ever.'

L ORD HANSON, the Yorkshire-born tycoon, together with his late partner Lord White, are rightly renowned for building Hanson plc into one of the United Kingdom's most successful industrial conglomerates. But he wasn't always part of the establishment.

Just as he got up the noses of industry rivals with his audacious business deals, so he doubtless ruffled a few feathers at Rolls-Royce.

Not for him any old common-or-garden Bentley: when Hanson caught sight of the sleek show car that Pininfarina built in 1968 based on a Bentley T-Series, he knew that his name was written all over it.

Quite apart from the Ferrari-like sloping roof, oblong headlamps and leather (rather than walnut) fascia, the car did away with a 'flying B' bonnet mascot. Terribly non-U, old boy.

Unique Bentley T-Series was built for Lord Hanson, who enjoyed 24,000km (15,000 miles) behind the wheel.

It was this car that inspired the later and uglier Rolls-Royce Camargue – a car that divided Rolls staff themselves into lovers and loathers of the Pininfarina design. Our captain of industry, meanwhile, loved it, covering almost 24,000km (15,000 miles) in it before selling the unique Bentley in 1979. At £225,000 at the time, the press christened it the most expensive used car ever – an epithet that probably made the shrewd Hanson chuckle.

Rapport Starlight

IN THE late 1970s the UK was the number one destination for wealthy Arabs hunting for something special to drive around in. With money no object, the aim was to get a motor car made that your neighbour, brother or royal rival hadn't got stashed away in his garage.

Many of the cars built as a consequence in railway arch workshops and air-freighted to Saudi Arabia and the United Arab Emirates were completely lashed up underneath their pearlescent paint.

And when sandstorms stripped panels back to shiny metal, or body parts warped under the fierce heat, or sills crudely made of timber offcuts dropped off, many of these unlikely creations were just abandoned in the sandy wilderness. It was time for another trip to the toyshop.

A lot of these customized cars were based on the Range Rover, with its Herculean separate chassis able to keep things straight. This unusual convertible, better made than most, was at least ingenious in grafting the front end of the contemporary Ford Granada on to the familiar Range Rover shape.

'Many of these unlikely creations were just abandoned in the sandy wilderness.'

It looks a bit like an ordinary minicab from the front, of course, but that doesn't matter: if this one's still going, that's probably what it's doing right now in Kuwait City.

Spot the difference: obviously, the convertible roof was something different from the standard-issue Range Rover, but so was the skillfully grafted-on Ford Granada front end . . .

Reliant Rebel

'It could easily manage 97km/h (60mph) and 21km/litre (60mpg).'

A REBEL THE first small four-wheeled Reliant certainly was. While large manufacturers poured millions of pounds into expensive development, the Rebel bucked the trend by mating a simple separate chassis to plastic bodywork, and equipping it with Reliant's own 600, then 700 and later 750cc all-aluminium engine.

Estate (below) and saloon (bottom) versions of the nippy and economical Rebel were offered by Reliant.

Reliant got around the problem of making a car with one more wheel than they usually required by tacking the entire independent front suspension structure from the Triumph Herald on to the trike's chassis frame.

The Rebel was not sophisticated. But . . . it could easily manage 97km/h (60mph) and 21km/litre (60mpg) even if it didn't have synchromesh on first gear.

Quality was patchy and the simple little renegade was never likely to topple the far more radical Mini small car from its pre-eminent position in popular affection. In nine years only about 3500 Rebel saloons and estates were built, and I can't remember the last time I saw one.

Rosengart Supertrahuit

'The average, war-weary Frenchman couldn't afford it.'

THE ROSENGART name could today have been up there with the likes of BMW and Nissan. Unlikely sounding, but true. All three began their car-making activities with none other than Britain's very own Austin Seven; Nissan in Yokohama, BMW in Munich and Rosengart just outside Paris. After the Model T Ford, the little car and Herbert Austin's licensing deals put the world on wheels.

After the Second World War, BMW had a terrible time and only survived by making bubble cars and motorbikes. Nissan built the latest Austin A40s in Oriental isolation. But Rosengart took a wrong turn in 1947 with this car, the Supertrahuit. It was a big, sporting, luxury machine with an American 3.9-litre Mercury V8 engine.

The average, war-weary Frenchman couldn't afford it – nor the punitive tax levied on such boulevardiers. Citroën introduced its small 2CV, Renault its 4CV, and both cleaned up.

Rosengart was in such dire straits that its response was effectively to re-introduce the by-now antediluvian 747cc, sidevalve-engined Austin Seven with a more modern body and call it the Ariette. It was a sales disaster and Rosengart, potentially France's very own BMW rival, went belly up.

After the ravages of the Second World War, the lavish Supertrahuit was not the car French motorists wanted.

Rover P6BS

'The car was designed to ride smoothly as well as handle like a dream.'

YOU'RE LOOKING at one of the greatest opportunities the British motor industry ever missed: the Rover P6BS. Here was an all-British, mid-engined and highly civilized supercar conceived a full quarter-century before Honda did the trick with its NSX.

Rover P6BS looks slightly ungainly (below) but had mid-mounted engine, visible under plastic 'bubble' (bottom).

The car was styled 'P6' because it was related to the Rover 2000 saloon of the same codename, 'B' for the Buick origins of its V8 engine and 'S' for sports car. The two-seater's engine was situated in front of the rear axle but behind the driver for perfect, racing car-style balance. Its SU carburettors were on display under a plastic 'dome' poking up through the engine cover.

The car was designed to ride smoothly as well as handle like a dream. The body, while at this stage only a roughly-hewn cover for the P6BS's high-tech innards, showed how low and neat a properly styled production car could be.

Rover bought the Alvis company in 1965 and intended to attach that touring car marque's name to the P6BS when it went on sale.

Alas, bitter and blinkered corporate infighting within the newly-formed British Leyland in 1968 conspired to kill this most exciting of British sports cars. The Jaguar faction opposed it because they knew it would sound the death knell for the E-Type; the Triumph camp did not want to jeopardize the yet-to-be-announced Stag.

The sole running prototype is one of the star exhibits at Rover's Heritage Centre at Gaydon, Warwickshire – a poignant reminder of when British cars took the first of many wrong turnings.

Scott Sociable

'There was no reverse on the three-speed gearbox.'

A LFRED ANGUS Scott is a motorbike folk hero. His distinctive Scott machines, made in Shipley, Yorkshire in the early years of the 20th century and bearing evocative names like Flying Squirrel, were nicknamed 'Yowling Two-Strokes' because of their rowdy, watercooled two-cylinder engines.

Scott incorporated one of these motors in a curious little three-wheeled vehicle he designed as a gun car for the First World War. When army chiefs gave it the bird, however, Scott decided to unleash it on the civilian world and, in 1919, it was launched as the Scott Sociable.

With two wheels at the back and the third offset to the driver's side at the front, the two-seater Sociable was built around a triangulated frame made from 43 straight tubes. It would have looked like some bizarre motorbike-and-sidecar, too, were it not for the fact that the polished wood-panelled, timber-framed bodywork appeared surprisingly streamlined and modern for the time. There was no reverse on the three-speed

Below: Room for two to squeeze into the Sociable.

Below: Three wheels on my wagon, but still rolling . . .

gearbox but the Sociable – so-called because driver and passenger were squashed in tightly together side-by-side – boasted a proper steering wheel and independent suspension.

So convinced was Alfred Scott that he was on to a winner, that he built a brand new factory to make the Sociable. But in 1922 the Austin Seven, truly a 'real car in miniature' was revealed. Scott died a year later. Despite its price being slashed from £273 to £135 in 1924, the Sociable flopped. About 110 were made and this one pictured, one of the five known survivors, can be seen today in Bradford's Industrial Museum. The Scott Sociable factory later became a print works and was demolished only recently.

Skoda Felicia

'It could be a treacherous handful' on rain-soaked roads.'

SKODA CELEBRATED its 100th birthday recently, at the same time as launching a massively improved version of its Favorit hatchback: the Felicia. Just as the Favorit evoked a long-forgotten Skoda of the 1930s, so the Felicia revived a name last used by the Czech car maker in 1964.

Cute 1950s styling but dodgy handling for the Felicia.

Skoda today refers to the old Felicia with all the affection and reverence that a company like Jaguar might use for the E-Type, or Porsche for the 356. So was it really such a great car?

Frankly, probably not. When introduced in 1958, the two-seater convertible Felicia was neither especially handsome nor particularly rapid, twin carburettors notwithstanding.

Its archaic separate chassis, swing axle rear suspension and tall, skinny wheels also meant it could be a treacherous handful on rain-soaked roads.

But what it did possess was a healthy appetite for tough and long service and the sort of pugnacious, comradely charm which may be destined today to be gradually squeezed out of Skoda by its new parent corporation Volkswagen.

The old Felicia, with some 16,000 made and a handful sold in England, stuck out like a sore thumb from its contemporaries. Today's certainly doesn't. With rose-tinted headlights, maybe that's exactly what Skoda wants these days.

Standard Vanguard Diesel

'Apart from being horribly noisy, the diesel Vanguard was tortoise-like.'

THERE IS not a mainstream car maker today without a diesel model in its range but, in the early 1950s, that simply was not the case. Just about the only one you could buy was a Mercedes – and even then it was only available almost exclusively in Germany.

Britain's first diesel car was born into this era, a ponderous, oil-burning version of the stodgy old Standard Vanguard.

Made by Standard and fitted to 30,000 of the Ferguson tractors it had made by then, the 2-litre lump of an engine necessitated a much stiffer chassis, while the four-speed gearbox got electric overdrive on second and top gears to help punt the car along.

Apart from being horribly noisy, the diesel Vanguard was tortoise-like – the wind would have to be in the right direction for the adventurous driver to beat 105km/h (65mph). Downhill.

The clattering, smelly promise of 18km/litre (50mpg) persuaded the Port Talbot Steel Works to run a large fleet of them in and around South Wales, but the car only lasted for two years (1954-55) and was not replaced.

If you followed one of these in the 1950s, the black smoke marked it out as a diesel – Britain's first.

Standard Vanguard Sportsman

'Sales, though, were terrible, at just 901 in two years.'

The Sportsman was actually meant to be a Triumph.

TODAY, CAR makers conjure up 'limited editions' simply by thinking of a breezy name, designing some stickers incorporating it to plaster on to a version of their staple products, installing a slightly better radio, and shouting the super low, low price from the rooftops.

The 1956 Standard Vanguard Sportsman would appear to be a primitive ancestor of such snappy sales techniques. But it most certainly isn't.

It's an uncomfortable reminder that Standard was, by this time, getting mighty uncomfortable with its name. Instead of implying regal flag-flying, 'Standard' was starting to be a metaphor for ordinary, dull, feature-less – bog, even.

This deluxe version of the Vanguard III saloon, with its unique grille, two-tone paintwork, twin carburettors and overdrive, was intended to carry the altogether more dynamic sounding

Triumph name – by then the property of the Standard Motor Co too.

The company got as far as ordering hundreds of Triumph radiator badges featuring an enamel globe for the car before its decision makers bottled out and decided to keep the Sportsman as Standard as possible.

Sales, though, were terrible, at just 901 in two years, perhaps because of the car's high £1231 price.

The dithering was over by 1963 when the Standard name, aged 60, was consigned to the archives and replaced forever by Triumph.

Startin Ford Galaxie 500 Hearse

'The Galaxie was one of the fastest cars then made in the US.'

THE NOBLE British hearse isn't known for its speed. Most cover minimal and hallowed local mileage at such a gentle pace that they last for years. Wily undertakers throughout the land often keep their lustrous black vehicles in sedate service for decade after decade, and it's not unusual for loved ones to make their final journey in a vehicle that is even older than they were.

For the true hearse-power enthusiast, what a way to go! This sombre vehicle was based on one of America's most powerful saloons, but actually built in Britain.

This 1963 hearse was built by one of the country's most eminent hearse manufacturers, Thomas Startin Junior of Aston, Birmingham, at a time when the traditional Austin Princess base car had become obsolete and the later Daimler limo wasn't yet available: it started life as a Ford Galaxie 500.

Nothing strange about that, you might think . . . until you remember that the Galaxie was one of the fastest cars then made in the US, and regularly thrashed such nimble sporting machines as Mini Coopers and Lotus Cortinas in saloon car racing in the hands of drivers like Jack Sears.

The racy 'ON 6' was bought by undertakers W.H. Scott and Son of Edgbaston, Birmingham in the very early 1960s and was still used by the firm until about 10 years ago, at which time it was scrapped and all of its useful mechanical components stripped to keep another Galaxie going. A shame, that.

All we can assume is that, for the sadly departed enthusiast, it was once the only way to go.

Steyr-Puch Haflinger

THE BRITISH Army has recently been evaluating an impressive six-wheel drive off-roader called a Pinzgauer as a replacement for its old Land-Rover ambulances. It's made in Austria by Steyr-Daimler-Puch, a little known company in the UK, but one that makes components for 40 per cent of the world's four-wheel-drive cars.

'In action, it was nothing short of incredible.'

And its pint-size ancestor, the Haflinger, also came to Britain in the 1960s and early '70s where it sold in small numbers to farmers with a technological bent.

The Haflinger was a tiny and ingeniously simple 4x4 utility vehicle with a 40bhp, 700cc, air-cooled, twin-cylinder engine at the back, differential locks at front and rear, and all-independent suspension.

Whether stripped down (right) or kitted-out (below), the Haflinger could attack tough terrain with gusto.

In appearance, the Haflinger was starkly industrial, with its basic pressed steel structure and canvas top. In action, it was nothing short of incredible, clattering its way up 50 degree slopes with gusto and scattering mud as it bounced across soggy farmland.

Far too utilitarian for today's 4x4 buyers, over 16,000 were made from 1959 until 1974. Most that came to Britain are probably still going strong, although, like the Mini Moke, the used Haflinger was a Bohemian favourite in the 1970s.

A British owners' club exists for survivors and is on the Internet – http:/www.ccc.nottingham.ac.uk/-ppzcad/haf.html.

Stimson Scorcher

ANY IDEA what this is? Britain's licensing authorities weren't exactly sure when they first clapped eyes on the Stimson Scorcher in 1976, and after some head-scratching they hesitatingly classified it as a motorcycle-sidecar combination.

By law that meant that both 'rider' and 'pillion' had to wear crash helmets, but the third occupant – the Scorcher seated three in a row – was legally the sidecar occupant and, thus, could ride bareheaded if he or she wanted to.

However, designer Barry Stimson, who designed the car in France, advised any trio of Scorcher occupants to wear 'skid-lids' because his outrageous trike, with Mini subframe, engine and gearbox at the front, could touch a giddy 161km/h (100mph) at full tilt.

The plastic body, on which driver and passengers sat astride, was made of glass fibre and the engine was completely exposed, hot-rod style – unless you plumped for the optional plastic bonnet.

A Brighton company called Noovoh Developments sold the Scorcher as a kit car for £385. It could be carried home on a normal roofrack before you set about making it. Only 30 Scorchers were made in four years of production and today, among the classic kit car cognoscenti, they're worth a small fortune.

'The engine was completely exposed, hot-rod style.'

The outrageous Stimson Scorcher could seat three in a row (below). It caused a sensation wherever is stopped (bottom, left) but the spare wheel would be easy to steal (bottom, right) if it was left unattended for long.

Studebaker Starlight Coupé

'Raymond Loewy was hired to shape these futuristic Studebakers.'

THE STUDEBAKER company was founded on making wagons and carts in the latter part of the 19th century, and was massively boosted by the demand for its wheelbarrows during the Californian gold rush. It made its first, electric, car in 1902 and rapidly developed into one of the largest car makers in America. But only in 1947 did Studebaker force its rivals to sit up and take notice.

The 1946 Studebakers led the world with their up-to-the-minute design.

Its innovative models, in two- and four-door Commander, Champion and Regal guises, were America's first totally new car design since 1941.

Their modern, forward-leaning looks, sleek lines and wraparound rear windows made contemporary vehicles seem geriatric by comparison. They benefited from some impressive outside influence: leading product designer Raymond Loewy was hired to shape these futuristic Studebakers. Underneath, though, things were trustworthy and reliable, based around Studebaker's all-iron straight-six engines.

If these cars were radical then the 1950 models, with their space-age 'bullet' nose styling – a massive circular 'grille' with a prominent chrome point bursting out of the centre and flanked by two chrome-surrounded air-intakes – were sensational. They helped Studebaker sell a record 320,884 cars that year.

From there, though, steady decline set in as the high wages the company paid and the location of its factories in Indiana and Ontario conspired to reduce

the company to a marginal force in the American motor industry's pecking order. The last Studebaker was made in 1966, and cars like this 1950 Champion Starlight coupé only live on in the hands of keen collectors.

Talbot Tagora

'The Tagora plummetted to the ground in record time.'

ONE DOLLAR: that's what France's Peugeot paid the Chrysler Corporation in 1978 when it bought the mammoth but financially crippled American car-maker's entire European operations. That did, of course, include all the debts and liabilities that went with it.

Slab-sided and unloved, the Tagora – here shown in its luxury SX guise – helped hasten the demise of Talbot.

It also included the assets: factories in Coventry, Scotland, France and Spain; the Sunbeam, Horizon, Avenger, Alpine and Solara models – yippee – and an image with all the prestige and fizz of a Rotherham bingo hall. And there, at the very bottom of the tea-chest, were the plans for Chrysler Europe's new executive car: the Tagora.

Under the revived name of Talbot the large, bluff-fronted saloon eventually emerged in 1981. Designed in Britain, and with either the asthmatic 2.2-litre engine from the old Chrysler 180 models or a hastily installed Peugeot 604 2.7 V6,

the Tagora had about as much aspirational appeal in the office car park, as the gatehouse that guarded it.

In the Great Lead Balloons of Our Time league, the Tagora plummetted to the ground in record time, selling a pathetic 23,400 in just under four years – that's about 16 cars a day across the whole of Europe. Middle management fleet-car drivers would have preferred even a base-model Ford Granada with vinyl seats and no radio to a top-notch Tagora with all the goodies.

The Talbot marque quietly expired not long afterwards. It had not been a dollar well spent.

Tickford Triumph Stag

'Discreet and tasteful, er, well . . . Expensive, definitely.'

WHEN ASTON Martin's Tickford engineering subsidiary set to work on this Triumph Stag in 1984, the car was already 10 years old. Its craftsmen blocked off the grille, fitted an aluminium airdam, a rear undertray and a boy racer bonnet bulge to make it look like an Aston Martin Vantage.

Then they flared the wheelarches to cover fat alloy wheels, and painted the car gleaming black – including the chrome bumpers – and tinted the windows to Ray-Ban levels of umbrage. It was the slickest-looking Stag ever.

The engine was modified to give a potent 200bhp while the interior was sumptuously retrimmed in Connolly leather seats and Wilton carpets.

Discreet and tasteful, er, well . . . Expensive, definitely: Tickford spent £20,000 on the car, around four times what a decent Stag was then worth.

The buyer, described simply as 'a northern motoring enthusiast', was so pleased with his customized Stag that he built a centrally-heated garage specially for it. Who he was or where the car is now remain a mystery.

Mean and moody black paint job, bonnet scoop and dramatic front air dam: the outward signs of £20,000 lavished on this Tickford-modified Stag.

Tornado Typhoon Sportsbrake

'Such homespun motor cars were deeply unfashionable.'

T HE KIT cars advertised in down-market DIY car magazines in 1950s' Britain offered a little bit of ersatz sophistication in a post-war era still gripped by austerity. The chassis and feeble engines of old Austin Sevens and Ford Populars could be laid bare and a new plastic body, invariably of a sporting nature, simply bolted on.

The Sportsbrake was probably the first sports-estate car.

Then most of the old instruments, seats and wheels could be 'replumbed' so that, after a weekend or two's hard graft in the shadow of the old air raid shelter, an enthusiastic amateur could create his own makebelieve Jaguar or Aston Martin for a price that was the equivalent of a few tanks of petrol for the real thing.

Such kit-cars were very much part of those make-do times.

Few offered much design finesse, so when the Tornado Typhoon Sportsbrake was launched in 1958 it caused a bit of a stir: its low-slung lines and useful opening tailgate married sports and estate car designs a full decade before the Reliant Scimitar GTE.

Alas, although there was also an open two-seater Typhoon, by the dawn of the 1960s and the advent of the Austin-Healey 'Frogeye' Sprite', such homespun motor cars were deeply unfashionable. Some 400 Typhoons were made in its four-year lifetime; and only a mere handful were Sportsbrakes.

Toyota Crown

'The car was a dismal no-hoper in the world's biggest car market.'

'TOYOTA' AND 'failure' are not words generally uttered in the same breath. Like sushi and French fries, they just don't go together. In 1957, however, the company, which a few decades earlier had been chiefly a maker of weaving looms, stared disaster in the face: 'Utter failure' is how even Toyota's official biographers, in unusually frank Jápanese style, describe it.

Toyota Crown of 1958 (bottom) fell apart when it hit American tarmac, but lessons learnt in the fiasco made the Corolla (below) a much more suitable US import.

Toyota, who had been making cars for home consumption since 1937, took its new Toyopet Crown Deluxe saloon to California, USA, in 1958 – confident that what up to 700 car-hungry Japanese were snapping up each month was bound to appeal to Americans as well.

Alas, faced with the long-distance, constant-speed driving of vast empty freeways – where Detroit's finest V8 iron burbled effortlessly along – the little 1.5-litre Crown was reduced to a rattling, overheated, gibbering wreck. Designed for the confines of a small island nation, the car was a dismal no-hoper in the world's biggest car market.

Toyota hastily withdrew and spent six soul-searching years designing and refining the small car it was convinced Americans *would* buy – the Corolla, which was launched in 1966. It has, of course, never looked back.

Triumph Silver Bullet

REMEMBER THAT 'sit-up-and-beg' convertible that TV's Channel Islands detective Bergerac drove around the lanes of Jersey? Well, it was a Triumph Roadster and the Silver Bullet was the all-British glamour wagon intended to replace it.

Announced in 1950, the Bullet, also known as the TR-X, boasted torpedo-like bodywork with enclosed rear wheels that was positively space-age in appearance beside the matronly Roadster.

Under this aluminium skin whirred a high-tech hornet's nest of hydraulics: the headlamps popped up electrically, as did the hood, windows, radio aerial and even the bonnet; the overdrive on the three-speed gearbox was also electro-hydraulically driven, and so were the seat adjustment controls.

An electric motor under the bonnet drove the system, which was carefully sandwiched inside the double-skinned aluminium bodywork.

But the Silver Bullet was bedevilled by problems. When it was demonstrated to Princess Margaret, none of the buttons matched the right functions and, when a prototype was out roadtesting one day, an engine fire broke out under the bonnet. This shorted the wiring, the power to open the bonnet was therefore lost, and the inextinguishable flames roared

'Flames roared unchecked inside until the car was completely burned out.'

unchecked inside until the car was completely burned out.

After this, the Silver Bullet plans were torn up and Triumph turned instead to the simple (and altogether less combustible) TR2 sports car. Only two of the three prototypes still survive.

Electric dreams: super-rare Silver Bullet in action today.

TVR Tina

'The Tina never made it into production.'

I F YOU'VE ever heard the raucous growl of a 5-litre TVR Griffith in traffic, or seen one roar past you on the motorway, you probably won't believe that this bland little sports car is from the same Blackpool-based engineering stable.

Early drawing of the Tina coupé by Trevor Fiore (below) was enticing; two-seater open roadster (bottom) looks attractive in 'the metal'. TVR ditched the Tina project due to high tooling costs for pressed-steel bodies.

The Tina was an ambitious idea to build a small TVR sports car using the floorpan of the Hillman Imp and is, in fact, the only TVR ever constructed with a steel body – all other TVRs have glass fibre 'clothing'.

Shown at the Earl's Court Motor Show in 1966, the car was styled by a Yorkshire designer originally called Trevor Frost, but who changed his name to the more exotic Trevor Fiore in order to attract more work from European car companies. His most well-known and prolific design work to date? The interior of the Renault 25 executive car.

But the sheer cost of putting a steel-bodied car into production – steel needs huge industrial presses to form it while

glass fibre can be made by hand in any old shed – meant that the Tina never made it into production. TVR instead

got on with making the unruly, high-powered hot-rods which have since made its name worldwide.

Vauxhall Equus

'The car remained a one-off styling exercise.'

THIS IS the Equus, which is Latin for horse, and unlike any other Vauxhall you're ever likely to see on the road. For anyone who thinks that the Triumph TR7 was a wedge-shaped ugly, then the Equus with its straight, angular lines and knife-edge profile, takes the form to another dimension altogether.

The Vauxhall Equus — the word is Latin for horse — could have ushered in a new dawn for British sports cars but plans to make it were cancelled. Interior (below) was neat and user-friendly; dart-like styling (bottom) the last from Vauxhall's now-defunct studio.

The time was 1978 and the Equus then represented the very latest in sports car design. Even so, it's hard to believe this car is now nearly 20 years old.

It also has the distinction of being the very last all-British-designed Vauxhall.

The Equus was widely tipped as an up-to-the-minute British successor to the MGB – an affordable sports car for everyone. And grandiose plans were drawn up to have it manufactured by Panther, on whose Lima sports car chassis the Equus was based.

But when Vauxhall's design department shut down in 1980, all Vauxhall development was transferred straight to Opel in Germany, and any

hopes lingering for such quintessentially British projects as the Equus were dashed. To howls of protest from the press, the car remained a one-off styling exercise.

Strangely, although Vauxhall makes much of its heritage, having recently opened a special collection of its heirlooms at Luton to the public, the Equus isn't a regular part of it and it barely merits a mention in Vauxhall's official company history book.

Volvo 480ES Convertible

'They decided to slice the top off to create a two-seater convertible.'

THE ANTIQUES trade swears by them, they line the leafy streets of London's Golder's Green and ply the highways and byways of the stockbroker belt, and caravans and horseboxes are usually pulled by them. But Volvos are not, by and large, fun cars.

Volvo came up with a particularly neat way of stowing the roof of its prototype 480ES convertible, but 'bottled out' when it came to offering it to the public. A Volvo soft-top, the C70, is now going on sale, however.

The closest the company has come to glamour is its classic P1800 coupé of the early 1960s. Even then, its stylish image was enhanced by accident: Roger Moore, as TV's Simon Templar in *The Saint*, drove one and instantly made white P1800s chic. Ironically the Volvo was

only used because Jaguar refused to lend producer Lew Grade an E-Type, 1961's other attractive new car.

Volvo's frustrated stylists, though, refused always to tow the sombre line. When the eminently sensible 480ES hatchback was unveiled in 1986, they

decided to slice the top off to create a two-seater convertible with an electrically-operated roof that any young blade would be proud to be seen in.

In 1991 Volvo tentatively announced that it would go into production but then, feeling perhaps that a convertible was just too frivolous for its sensible image, the car was cancelled at the last minute, and Volvo PR men hastily changed the subject whenever the matter of Volvo's elusive roadster was raised.

Now, however, a big new Volvo coupé and convertible are on the stocks with major British design input from Oxfordshire's TWR. Could it be that, sideboards, synagogues and showjumpers notwithstanding, Volvo is about to change forever?

Wallis Special

'An ace bomber pilot had little spare time for such Wooster-ish transport.'

KNOW YOUR James Bond films and you'll know who this is pictured towering over the car. No? Ken Wallis ring any bells? Wing Commander Ken Wallis is, in fact, a leading exponent of the autogyro, a cross between a microlight aircraft and a helicopter. One of these, 'Little Nellie', helped 007 outwit and shoot down his pursuers in *You Only Live Twice*.

Before the Second World War, when Wallis was a fearless airborne hero in Lysanders and Wellington bombers, his passion was cars. He turned a £25 Bentley 3-litre into a racy two-seater, but this waist-height roadster was his idea of how a perfect rakish sports car should look in the mid-1930s.

It featured two overlapping Austin Seven chassis, with the end of the front one turned upwards to facilitate better steering, and an Austin Seven engine.

He made the entire body himself from aluminium and, so that nothing would spoil its lines, even hid its special French Marchal headlamps behind a curved grille set low between the front wheels.

An ace bomber pilot had little spare time for such Wooster-ish transport, though, and the car was sold in 1945. What happened to it Wallis doesn't know. In the 1950s he built an even more impressive Rolls-Royce-based special, in which he toured the USA while on RAF service.

In 1964 Wallis quit the Force to develop his autogyros full-time. He flew Little Nellie for the stunt scenes in the Bond film and until recently – aged 79 – Wallis regularly took to the air from his home in Norfolk.

Ken Wallis and the incredible sports car he created.

Weitz X600

'He chose England as the place to turn his dream car into reality.'

JOHN WEITZ was one of the first men to appear on the International Best-Dressed List (compiled by Eleanor Lambert, PR executive and journalist) in 1967, one of the many gems on his amazingly impressive CV that makes him a sickeningly high achiever compared to mere mortals like ourselves.

Clothes designer, author of best-selling novels, photographer, ex-US Army Intelligence officer recently accorded Commander rank in the Order of Merit of the German Republic, he splits his time between London, New York and Tokyo while presiding over his exclusive worldwide fashion business.

But his one car design, the X600, was an uncharacteristic low-point in an otherwise sparkling career; the grand plan to make 1000 replicas never got even close to realization.

Berlin-born émigré Weitz was educated at St. Paul's School, London and Oxford. He was also a keen amateur racing driver. So he chose England as the place to turn his dream car into reality – employing a maker of vintage Bentley copies called Derry Mallalieu at Wootton, Oxfordshire – in 1979.

Based on a Chevrolet Camaro Z28 chassis, the swoopy X600 was aluminium-clothed and resembled an Austin-Healey 3000 crossed with the Batmobile. 'I commuted every weekend for six months,' says Weitz, 'Concorde to and fro, to get this thing done'.

But when Mallalieu was wound up after its founder's death, the X600 went no further. While John Weitz still sits at his drawing board at 500 Madison Avenue, X600 lies long forgotten in a Cleveland aircraft museum.

Weitz guy: John and X600 under Manhattan's Queensboro' bridge (below). The X600's beak (opposite).

Above: Tail view of X600 shows it in a rather more rakish light; picture taken outside the Imperial Palace in Tokyo, with Weitz dapper as ever. Below: To the Batmobile — let's go!

Winchester

'It boasted one innovation: a single-piece plastic body.'

CHALLENGERS TO the traditional London taxi, made in Coventry by an organization called London Taxis International, are few and far between, so the city's cabbies were naturally curious when Winchester Automobiles (West End) Ltd unveiled this slab-sided creation in 1963 for their appraisal.

Wintry launch day for the Winchester taxi, notable for its plastic bodywork, recessed light in the door sill, and conspicuous unpopularity among London's cabbies. .

Although the Winchester was slow, heavy at 1380kg (3042lb) and underpowered with only a 1.6-litre diesel engine, it boasted one innovation: a single-piece plastic body. Made of Cellobond, as its manufacturer announced proudly.

If your Winchester was struck a blow by another vehicle, its Cellobond body could be repaired in four hours using

nothing more, it was claimed, than 'glass fibre mat, resin, catalyst, accelerator, Sellotape and tin foil'.

Other novelties included an illuminated step for the rear passenger doors, and a sign that read 'Taxi For Hire' instead of just plain 'Taxi'.

But none of it endeared the Winchester to London's sceptical taxi drivers, and nor did a later switch to Ford

Cortina petrol engines to tempt the provincial driver. This choice of powerplant did make the Winchester popular with film location and prop men, though – diesel engines interfered badly with contemporary sound equipment.

In almost 10 years of production, Winchester managed to sell just one cab a fortnight. The next new taxi, the Metrocab, didn't arrive until 1987.

Yugo Sana

'Critics in 1989 found it reasonable to drive, if a little rough around the edges.'

War victim? Hostilities helped ruin Sana's chances.

'THE CHEAPEST new car in America' was a proud boast that turned sour very fast for its Yugoslavian maker in the 1980s. Sales of the Yugo 55, an ugly hatchback, only Rover Metro-size, were initially brisk, as blue-collar America jostled for a spanking new 'compact' in exchange for just a fistful of dollars. But the car's quality and reliability was so dire that irate customers soon clamoured for their money back.

Instead of returning the greenbacks, Yugo's solution was a new car, called the Florida in an attempt to woo a disenchanted American market. Well, not totally new, since much of its mechanical hardware was shared with the Italian Fiat Tipo, but it did at least possess a neat, new, five-door body, styled by Ital Design.

Quality was vastly improved, claimed the factory, but prices, punters were glad to hear, were still rock bottom.

Critics in 1989 found it reasonable to drive, if a little rough around the edges. It was sold in the UK as the Yugo Sana.

But the civil war that erupted in what was, by then, Serbia effectively ended any hopes of international success as exports were abruptly terminated. Certainly, no self-respecting Croatian or Bosnian would wish to be seen behind the wheel of what was, anyway, an extraordinarily lacklustre motor car.

Zagato Z-Eco

'Its two passengers would sit in tandem under a canopy on one side of the car.'

FIAT KNEW deep down that its baby Cinquecento was spot-on for the 1990s. Why else would it invite eight independent design houses to try and better it? The debut of the new '500' in 1992 was accompanied by a flotilla of specially commissioned 'concept cars' based on its mechanical parts and dimensions.

There were the predictable small coupés, buggies and estates, and this curiosity, the Zagato Z-Eco.

Venerable Italian coachbuilder Zagato, famed for its dashing lightweight sports car bodies for Alfa Romeo and Lancia, reasoned that this would be the ideal car for commuting to work.

Its two passengers would sit in tandem under a canopy on one side of the car, as on a motorbike, while an adult-size bicycle stood fixed upright on the other.

Zagato thought it had come up with the perfect answer to 1990s commuting with its nifty Z-Eco, one of a series of Fiat Cinquecento-based concept cars.

When the traffic ground to a halt, the Z-Eco would be parked in the nearest suburban avenue and one of its occupants would grab the bike and carry on pedalling to the office.

But even that wouldn't be too strenuous an exercise, because the bike also incorporated an electric motor, which recharged while it was on board the car and plugged in, and so was ready whenever needed.

The Z-Eco, though, never actually turned a wheel – the bike was real even if the show car was made of plaster. Such a shame: getting a bike into a normal Cinquecento is well nigh impossible.

Index